IMPRESSUM

Das Buch zum Film "B-Movie: Lust & Sound in West-Berlin"
von Jörg A. Hoppe, Klaus Maeck, Heiko Lange

Edel Books
Ein Verlag der Edel Germany GmbH
A division of Edel Germany GmbH

Copyright © 2015 Edel Germany GmbH,
Neumühlen 17, 22763 Hamburg
www.edel.com

Herausgeber / Publisher: Jörg A. Hoppe
Projektkoordination / Project management: Dr. Marten Brandt
Redaktion / Editor: Hollow Skai
Layout und Umschlaggestaltung / Layout and jacket design: Stefan „Doktor" Schmitz
Bildredaktion / Picture desk: Hollow Skai
Übersetzung / Translation: Jennifer D. Lew Schneider

Titelfoto / Title Photographer: Kain Karawahn

Druck und Bindung / Printing and binding:
optimal media GmbH, Glienholzweg 7, 17207 Röbel / Müritz

Alle Rechte vorbehalten. All rights reserved.

Das Werk darf – auch teilweise – nur mit Genehmigung des
Verlages wiedergegeben werden.
This book is sold subject to the condition that it shall not,
by way of trade or otherwise, be lent, resold, hired out, or
otherwise circulated without the publisher´s prior consent
in any form of binding or cover other than that in which it
is published and without a similar condition, including this
condition, being imposed on the subsequent purchaser.

Printed in Germany

ISBN 978-3-8419-0385-3

BOOK

Von Mark Reeder
Aufgeschrieben von Hollow Skai
und herausgegeben von Jörg A. Hoppe

By Mark Reeder
Written down by Hollow Skai
and published by Jörg A. Hoppe

INHALT

POPMUSIK & ZEITVERTREIB
[9]

**I.
A ONE-WAY-TICKET**
[17]

**II.
KOMAKINO**
[47]

**III.
KALTES KLARES WASSER**
[55]

**IV.
DER KRIEG GEGEN DEN SCHLAF**
[79]

**V.
DU BIST AUF SENDUNG**
[111]

**VI.
EIN SCHICKSAL NAMENS MONIKA**
[145]

**VII.
DE-MILITARISIERUNG DER MODE**
[157]

**VIII.
DISNEYLAND FÜR DEPRESSIVE**
[169]

**IX.
BUM, BUM, BUM**
[187]

DIE MITWIRKENDEN
[205]

BILDNACHWEIS
[224]

CONTENTS

POP MUSIC AND PASTIME
[9]

I. A ONE-WAY-TICKET
[17]

II. KOMAKINO
[47]

III. KALTES KLARES WASSER
[55]

IV. THE WAR AGAINST SLEEP
[79]

V. YOU'RE ON THE TELLY
[111]

VI. A FATE CALLED MONIKA
[145X]

VII. DEMILITARISATION OF FASHION
[157]

VIII. DISNEYLAND FOR DEPRESSIVES
[169]

IX. BOOM, BOOM, BOOM
[187]

THE CONTRIBUTORS
[205]

PICTURE CREDITS
[224]

POPMUSIK UND ZEITVERTREIB
POPMUSIC AND PASTTIME

VORWORT VON / FOREWORD BY
JÖRG A. HOPPE

◄ ▼ Blixa Bargeld, ▼ Günter Thews und Jörg A. Hoppe (rechts), ▼ Farin Urlaub (2. Reihe links), Hunter & Stefan Kleinkrieg von Extrabreit und Gudrun Gut, ▼ Feuerschlucker Paul Busch
► MC-Cover *Sleep?*, ▼ Gudrun Gut

Wenn Ilse Ruppert nicht an Bord des Ausflugdampfers Seute Deern gewesen wäre und alle meine Gäste fotografiert hätte, wahrscheinlich hätte ich mich fast drei Jahrzehnte später gar nicht mehr an meinen Geburtstag 1984 erinnern können. Und wenn sie mir nicht 27 Jahre später ein Album mit diesen Fotos geschenkt hätte, wäre ich wahrscheinlich nie auf die Idee gekommen, den Film *B-Movie* zu machen.

Bilder sind wie Schlüssel. Sie öffnen etwas Verborgenes, die Erinnerung an einen besonderen Moment und die damit verbundenen Gefühle – oder eine neue, fremde Welt, die unmittelbar und direkt wirkt. Werber sprechen von „the magic bullet", von Schüssen direkt ins Gehirn. Genau so wirken gute Bilder. Und diese Fotos waren wie ein Film, der plötzlich vor meinen Augen abzulaufen begann.

1984 hatte ich mit Gudrun Gut ein kleines Büro in der Wittelsbacher Straße 18 in West-Berlin: Kartell – Popmusik und Zeitvertreib. Wir hatten gerade mehrere Kartons mit unserer MC-Compilation *SLEEP? west berlin 1984 unvollständige bestandsaufnahme* an musikinteressierte Japaner verkauft, die auch noch bar bezahlten. Auf dem Cassettensampler waren u.a. Die Tödliche Doris, La Loora, Mannamaschine, Die Haut, Hacke Experience, VOOV, Mata D'Or, Frieder Butzmann und Blixa Bargeld mit *Der morgige Tag ist mein*.

Ich liebte dieses Lied. Das war Berlin. Mein West-Berlin.

Gudrun hatte die Idee mit dem Spreedampfer, der an diesem trüben Septemberabend in Tegel um 21 Uhr ablegte. Eine ungewöhnlich frühe Zeit für Berliner Partys, die meist erst um Mitternacht begannen. So verpassten viele die Abfahrt. Jim Rakete zum Beispiel. Und wohl auch Mark Reeder, der auf keinem der Fotos zu finden ist. Mark war 1984 mit seiner neuen Band Shark Vegas als Vorgruppe von New Order auf Europa-Tournee gewesen und hatte mit Muriel Gray ein Berlin-Special für das englische Fernsehen gedreht, aus dem es auch Sequenzen in *B-Movie* gibt.

If Ilse Ruppert hadn't been on board the excursion steamer and hadn't photographed all my guests, perhaps three decades later I would have never been able to remember my birthday party from 1984 at all. And if she hadn't sent me an album with these photographs 27 years later, I probably would never have had the idea of making the film *B-Movie*.

Pictures are like keys. They reveal something hidden away: both the memory of a special moment and the feeling wrapped up in that moment – perhaps a new, strange world that seems immediate and real. Advertisers speak of "the magic bullet", shots directly into the brain. Good pictures have exactly this effect. And these photographs were like a film that suddenly began to play out before my eyes.

In 1984, I shared a small office with Gudrun Gut on Wittelsbacher Straße 18 in West Berlin: Kartell – Pop music and Pastime. We had just sold several boxes of our MC-compilation *SLEEP? west berlin 1984 unvollständige bestandsaufnahme* (incomplete inventory) to Japanese music dilettantes who paid us in cash. On the cassette sampler were, among others, Die Tödliche Doris, La Loora, Mannamaschine, Die Haut, Hacke Experience, VOOV, Mata D'Or, Frieder Butzmann and Blixa Bargeld with "Der morgige Tag ist mein" (Tomorrow belongs to me).

I loved this song. It was Berlin. My West Berlin.

Gudrun had the idea for the excursion steamer that set off on that overcast September evening in Tegel at 9 p.m. It was an unusually early time for the start of a party in Berlin since most parties would begin around midnight. That's why many people missed the departure time. Like Jim Rakete. And Mark Reeder, too, who can't be found in any of the photos. Mark was on tour in 1984 with his new band, Shark Vegas, as the opening band for New Order, on tour in Europe, and he, along with Muriel Gray, had filmed a Berlin special for British television, clips of which can be seen in *B-Movie*.

Ein Haufen Hedonisten und Musiker, Darsteller und Selbstdarsteller, Künstler und Lebenskünstler hatte sich eingefunden, und alle wollten feiern. Auch der Käpt'n. Den hatte Nena schon nach kurzer Zeit mit einer Flasche Jägermeister so abgefüllt, dass nicht länger sicher war, ob wir je wieder das Ufer erreichen würden.

Nena hatte mit *99 Red Balloons* gerade einen Mega-Monster-Welthit. Auch Die Ärzte waren gut drauf, wie man auf den Fotos sieht. Sie hatten ihre erste Platte *Uns geht's prima* veröffentlicht und den Film *Ritchie Guitar* gedreht, in dem auch Nena mitspielt und aus dem in *B-Movie* ebenfalls Ausschnitte zu sehen sind. Die Tödliche Doris mit Tabea Blumenschein sorgte 1984 mit ihrer Box *Chöre und Soli* für Furore und hatte auf Helgoland einen gleichnamigen Film gedreht, in dem auch Blixa Bargeld mitspielt. Die Einstürzenden Neubauten arbeiteten an ihrem Meisterwerk *½ Mensch*, das ihnen schon bald zum internationalen Durchbruch verhalf. Der junge WestBam alias Westfalia Bambaataa hatte seine erste Platte *17 – This Is Not A Boris Becker Song* veröffentlicht und war nun auch Haus-DJ im Metropol am Nollendorfplatz. Er war bei Kartell unter Vertrag, und wir hatten gerade mit ihm und Gudruns Freundinnen von Malaria! ein Video gedreht; auch dieses ist Teil des Films *B-Movie*.

Auf einem der Party-Fotos bin auch ich zu sehen. Ich sitze dort neben Günter Thews von den Anarcho-Spaß-Guerillas Die 3 Tornados. Günter erklärte mir Aids und HIV und dass es auch schon eine Berliner Aids-Hilfe gäbe. Es war das einzige Gespräch, an das mich noch erinnern kann. Und ich ahnte: The end is coming soon.

Also tanzten wir weiter auf dem Vulkan. Fünf Jahre später war unser West-Berlin Geschichte.

Danke Ilse, danke allen, die die Zeit für einen Moment für uns festgehalten haben.

A shitload of hedonists and musicians, actors and exhibitionists, artists and thrill-seekers had found each other, and they all wanted to party. The Cap'n, too. Nena had, in short order, given him so much Jägermeister that it wasn't clear if we would make it back to shore.

Nena had just made her mega-monster-world-wide hit with "99 Red Balloons". The Ärzte were also stoked, as one can see from the photos. They had just released their first album, *Uns geht's prima,* and made their first film, Ritchie Guitar - which also featured Nena – clips from which can also be seen in B-Movie. Die Tödliche Doris with Tabea Blumenschein created a furore in 1984 with their green box Chöre und Soli, and had just shot a film on Helgoland, appropriately named Helgoland, featuring Blixa Bargeld. The group Die Einstürzenden Neubauten were working on their masterpiece ½ Mensch which was about to help them make their international breakthrough. The young WestBam a.k.a. Westfalia Bambaataa had just released his first LP *17 – This Is Not a Boris Becker Song* and was now working as the resident-DJ at Metropol on Nollendorfplatz. He was signed at Kartell and we had just shot a video with him and Gudrun's girlfriends from Malaria!; clips from this are also part of the film *B-Movie*.

I also appear on one of the party photos. I am sitting next to Günter Thews of the anarchist spassguerilla group Die 3 Tornados. Günter explained to me all about AIDS and HIV and that there was already a Berlin AIDS help group. That is the only conversation that I can remember. And I had a premonition: the end is coming soon.

So we continued to dance on the edge of the smoking volcano. Five years later, the West Berlin we knew was just a memory.

Thank you Ilse, thank you to everyone, for capturing that brief moment of time for us.

◀▲ Der wahre Heino mit Blixa Bargeld und
▼ mit WestBam
▶▲ Bela B (Mitte) und Farin Urlaub von Die Ärzte,
▶ Wolfgang Müller (rechts),
▼ Nena und Gudrun Gut

A ONE-WAY-TICKET

MANCHESTER — BERLIN

Mein Name ist Mark Reeder und meine Geschichte von West-Berlin beginnt in Manchester.

Ende der Siebzigerjahre war die Stadt, in der die Industrielle Revolution einst ihren Anfang genommen hatte, potthässlich. Ein Streik folgte auf den anderen. Eine Fabrik nach der anderen machte dicht, und die Aussichten waren finster. Manchester lag am Boden und die Mancs waren arm und verzweifelt.

Aber es war meine Heimat, und die Stadt hat mich und vor allem meinen Musikgeschmack geprägt. Mit 14 hatte ich angefangen, samstags in einem kleinen Plattenladen in der Lever Street zu jobben. Bevor er zu Manchesters Punk-Mekka wurde, war er ein Hippie-Plattenladen, in dem ständig Räucherstäbchen glimmten, damit es nicht so sehr nach Gras und Haschisch roch. Der Virgin Record Shop war eine Insel der Seligen, wo man sich mit den neuesten Sounds aus aller Welt zudröhnen konnte. Weil die Kopfhörer ständig geklaut wurden oder kaputt waren, hatten wir in die Kopfstützen einer Sitzbank billige Lautsprecher eingebaut, sodass sich alles zu einem infernalischen Soundbrei vermischte, wenn mehrere Leute gleichzeitig in neue Platten reinhörten. Nach der Schule studierte ich Werbegrafik, doch schon bald schmiss ich meinen Job in einer Agentur und arbeitete full time im Virgin Shop, dem musikalischen Epizentrum von Manchester. So konnte ich den ganzen Tag Musik hören und wurde auch noch dafür bezahlt. Perfekt.

Dort hörte ich in den 70ern auch zum ersten Mal das, was in England als *Krautrock* bezeichnet wurde. Platten von NEU!, Amon Düül, Harald Großkopf, Cluster, Can und Popol Vuh oder von Elektronikpionieren wie Kraftwerk, Klaus Schulze und Tangerine Dream. Das war auch meine Chill-out-Musik nach einem anstrengenden Arbeitstag, an dem hauptsächlich Punk Rock und Reggae gespielt wurden. Diese deutschen Bands schielten nicht auf einen schnellen Chart-Erfolg und machten nicht auf Teufel komm raus Popmusik. Synthesizer wurden damals in England nur von bekannten Bands wie Yes oder King Crimson eingesetzt, weil sie so teuer waren, und 15 Minuten lange Tracks gab es sonst höchstens von Pink Floyd oder Rick Wakeman. Die kompromisslose Musik dieser deutschen

My name is Mark Reeder and my story about West Berlin begins in Manchester.

By the end of the seventies, the city that had once been the beating heart of the industrial revolution was suffering a cardiac arrest, it had become an ugly, poor and desperate place. The entire country was plagued with constant general strikes and factories were closing down one after the other, the future looked very grim. Most people were looking at a bleak future of boredom and misery. Thankfully though, because of this particular situation, I was spared a lifetime of grueling hard labor on a filthy factory floor. I studied advertising art and graphic design, when it was literally cut and paste. You would constantly be on the look-out for E's… on a sheet of Letraset. But Manchester was my home and the city that had shaped me and – above all – my taste in music. At the age of 14, I had started working Saturdays at a small Virgin record shop on Lever Street. Before it became Manchester's Punk Mecca, it was more of a hippie record shop that stank of incense which could always be found burning to disguise the smell of grass and hashish. This record shop was like an island for the blessed, where music junkies could absorb the latest sounds from around the globe.

Sure, I tried working in a few ad agencies, but I realised it just wasn't me. I hated it. So I left to work in the place where I already spent most of my free time and money, in Virgin's little record shop.

The Virgin record shop was the musical epicentre of Manchester. Here I could listen to music all day long and get paid for it. The Perfecct job. Well, almost.

Because our headphones constantly got stolen or broken, we constructed a lush seating area with headrests, in which very cheap loudspeakers were installed. Of course, when more than one person listened to music at the same time - which was usually the case - all you could hear was an infernal din.

It was in this little shop that I'd first heard a sound of music from Germany called *Krautrock*. These were obscure German import records from bands such as NEU!, Amon Düül, Cosmic Jokers, Cluster, Can and Popol Vuh, or from electronic pioneers like Kraftwerk, Klaus Schulze and

▶ Mark Reeder, 1979

Gruppen elektrisierte mich, und so wurde ich schon bald zum Krautrock-Experten. Wenn jemand eine durchsichtige Vinylscheibe von Faust oder Platten von Michael Rother, Ash Ra Tempel oder den Cosmic Jokers suchte, die damals sehr schwer zu beschaffen waren, kam er zu mir in den Laden.

Mit Manchester ging es jedoch immer mehr den Bach runter. Und so lebte fast jeder von der Stütze, machte Musik und hoffte, einen Plattenvertrag zu ergattern; jedenfalls jeder, den ich kannte. Den Stein ins Rollen brachte dabei das erste Konzert der Sex Pistols außerhalb von London. Als sie am 4. Juni 1976 in der Lesser Free Trade Hall auftraten, standen sowohl Pete Shelley und Howard Devoto von den Buzzcocks im Publikum, die das Konzert organisiert hatten, als auch Mark E. Smith (The Fall), Peter Hook und Bernard Sumner von Joy Division, Morrissey (The Smiths) und der TV-Moderator und Gründer von Factory Records, Tony Wilson, sowie Paul Morley, der später Frankie Goes To Hollywood groß rausbrachte. Die Sex Pistols wiesen uns den Weg in die Zukunft und zeigten uns, dass man nur als Musiker eine Chance hatte, dem Elend zu entfliehen.

Ich selbst spielte kurz darauf Bass in der Punkband The Frantic Elevators, die sich aber schon bald wieder auflöste, obwohl wir sogar mal im Vorprogramm von Sham 69 aufgetreten waren; unser Sänger Mick Hucknall sollte später mit Simply Red deutlich mehr Erfolg haben.

In den Siebzigerjahren kannten die meisten Engländer Deutschland nur aus dem Fernsehen, aus Spielfilmen mit bösen Nazis und aus Dokumentationen über den Zweiten Weltkrieg. Diese Bilder übten auf uns Kids jedoch eine große Faszination aus. Und als der Punk uns mit voller Wucht traf, zog manch einer von uns eine billige Uniformjacke oder -hose an oder trug sogar ein Hakenkreuz, um unsere Alten zu provozieren.

Deutschland und insbesondere Berlin war für uns ein Mysterium. Wir wussten eigentlich nichts über Berlin, außer dass Lou Reed ein Album veröffentlicht hatte, das so hieß. Doch lebten dort nicht Klaus Schulze und Edgar Froese von Tangerine Dream? Und hatte es nicht auch David Bowie und Iggy Pop in die Mauerstadt

Tangerine Dream. This became my chill-out music after a hard day at work, where reggae and punk rock played all day. I noticed these German bands were not focused on making commercial records, nor making chart-topping pop music like we were. Back then in England, synthesizers were very expensive and used mainly by progressive rock bands such as Yes and King Crimson, Pink Floyd or Rick Wakeman, who had tracks that were 15 minutes long. The reactionary music of these German groups electrified me – and soon, I became quite a Krautrock expert. Indeed, when someone was looking for a transparent vinyl record from Faust or records from Michael Rother, Ash Ra Tempel or the Cosmic Jokers, which were really hard to find at that time, they came to me at the shop. I too became infeceted with German import disease.

At this time Manchester however, was struggling to survive. Almost everyone was on the dole, or making music in the hope of getting a recording contract and making a hit. At least everybody I knew made music. The event that really set the punk rock ball rolling, was the first concert by The Sex Pistols outside of London. When they appeared on stage at the Lesser Free Trade Hall in June 1976, not only the organisers of the gig, Pete Shelley and Howard Devoto - from the Buzzcocks - were in the audience, but also a crowd of initiates who were destined to create great things, Mark E. Smith (The Fall), Peter Hook and Bernard Sumner from Joy Division, Mick Hucknall (Simply Red), Jon The Postman, Morrissey (The Smiths) and the TV presenter and founder of Factory Records Tony Wilson, as well as Paul Morley, who would later discover Frankie Goes To Hollywood. The Sex Pistols pointed the way into the future, showing us that the only way to escape the misery around us, was to become a musician. I was also enthused and played bass guitar for a while in a punk band called *The Frantic Elevators* which eventually broke up, even though we supported Sham 69. Our singer, Mick Hucknall, would later come to have slightly more success with his next band, Simply Red.

In the seventies, most Brits only knew Germany from war films on the telly, showing evil Nazi Germany or documentaries about World War II. These pictures,

verschlagen, wo Brian Eno ihre Platten in den Hansa Studios produzierte? Als ich Manchester und meinem kleinen Plattenladen den Rücken kehrte, um nach West-Berlin zu fahren, fragte mich Pete Shelley von den Buzzcocks denn auch, ob ich David Bowie treffen wolle. Meine Eltern und insbesondere unsere Nachbarn konnten hingegen nicht verstehen, dass ich unbedingt nach Deutschland wollte. Meine Mutter hatte die deutschen Bombenangriffe auf Manchester im Zweiten Weltkrieg noch in guter Erinnerung und damals Tragflächenspitzen für die Lancaster-Bomber gebaut, die wiederum Berlin bombardierten. Doch ich war total neugierig auf die Stadt, die weit hinter dem Eisernen Vorhang lag, der West- von Ost-Europa trennte. Und natürlich auf die Musik, die von dort kam und so anders klang — radikal, kompromisslos und wie von einem anderen Stern. Ich freute mich darauf, all diese seltenen elektronischen Krautrock-Platten zu finden, die in England nicht erhältlich waren. Das war mein größter Anreiz.

Die Reise nach Berlin war allerdings ein ziemliches Abenteuer. Damals gab es noch keine Billig-Airlines, als Normalsterblicher musste man schon mit dem Auto oder dem Motorrad fahren, um von Westdeutschland aus dorthin zu gelangen. Oder mit der Bahn. Ich hatte ein Billigticket, mit dem man überall in Europa reisen konnte, und begab mich auf eine Tour, die mich nach Düsseldorf, Köln, Frankfurt, München und Hamburg führte. Düsseldorf fand ich interessant, Hamburg auch, aber Berlin zog mich irgendwie magisch an.

Zunächst musste ich jedoch das rote Meer überqueren. Weil ich meinen Anschlusszug verpasst hatte, trampte ich dorthin. Die DDR schien riesengroß zu sein, zumindest schien die mehrstündige monotone Fahrt auf der unbeleuchteten und ruckeligen Transitstrecke kein Ende zu nehmen, und was ich erblickte, sah ziemlich finster aus. Ich sprach kein Deutsch und konnte gerade mal „Hände hoch!" und „Achtung!" sagen, was leicht missverstanden werden konnte, wenn ich Brötchen kaufen wollte. Auf der Transitstrecke durch die DDR hörten wir einen nervigen Signalcode der Alliierten im Radio, der mir wie ein Spionagesender vorkam, weil er nonstop Zifferncodes

however, fascinated us. As punk rock hit us with full force, we experimented with an appropriate fashion, throwing off all we had known before, but as we were living on the borderline of poverty, we were forced to adapt what we had. To express our distaste, we drain-piped our flares, ravaged our school uniforms and rebuilt them with safety pins, some of us even wore cheap military jackets or trousers and a few provocatively wore swastika arm bands in order to piss off their parents.

Certainly, Germany was still *the enemy*, and especially Berlin was a complete mystery to us. In fact, we knew virtually nothing about Berlin except that Lou Reed had made an album with the same name and that it was apparently a depressive, grim, grey and very inhospitable place. But then again, it must have had some attaction, didn't Klaus Schulze and Edgar Froese from Tangerine Dream live there? And hadn't David Bowie and Iggy Pop lost themselves in the walled city, producing their finest records at Hansa Studios? As I prepared to leave Manchester and my little record shop for the enigma of West Berlin, Pete Shelley from the Buzzcocks, curious as to my intentions, asked me if I was hoping to meet David Bowie there.

My parents, and especially our neighbours couldn't understand why I wanted to go to Germany. My mother could clearly remember the German blitz attacks on Manchester in World War II, and she herself had worked in the armaments industry at Avro's, rivetting the wingtips of Lancaster bombers which were used to bomb Berlin, but I was curious about this divided city that lay deep within an iron curtain country, the place where east met west in the middle of Eastern Europe. And of course, I was curious about the music I would find there too, which I knew would sound completely different to anything we had in Britain. I was looking forward to discovering all these obscure electronic Krautrock records that weren't available in England. That was like a magnet, drawing me in. Getting to Berlin was in itself quite an adventure. Back then, there weren't any cheap airlines. For the mortal majority, you had to travel from West Germany by car or by motor bike, or by train. As a 20 year old, I had a cheap train ticket

▶ ▲ Screenshots B-Movie:
Virgin Record Shop in Manchester,
▼ Mark Reeder vor dem Risiko

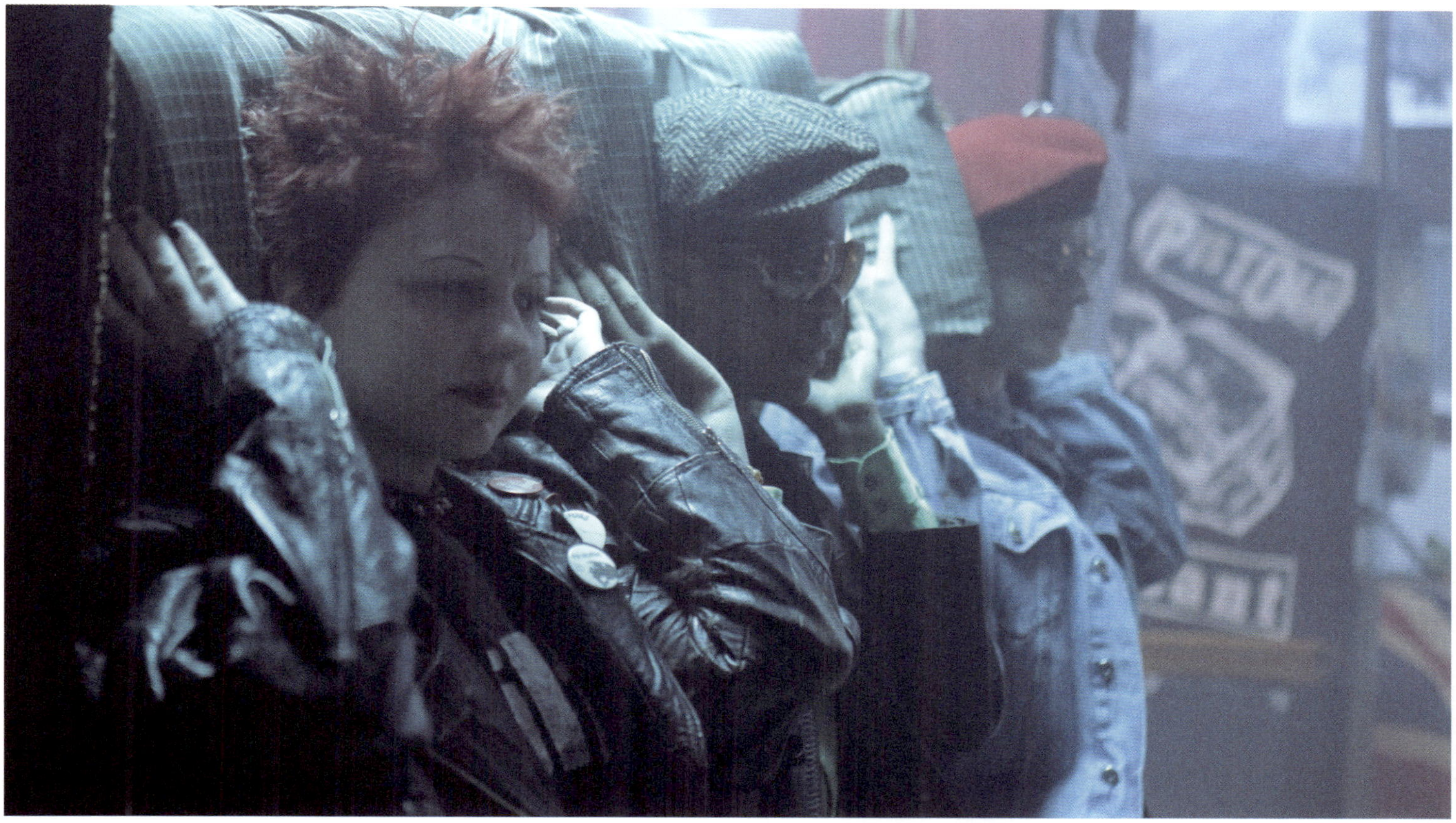

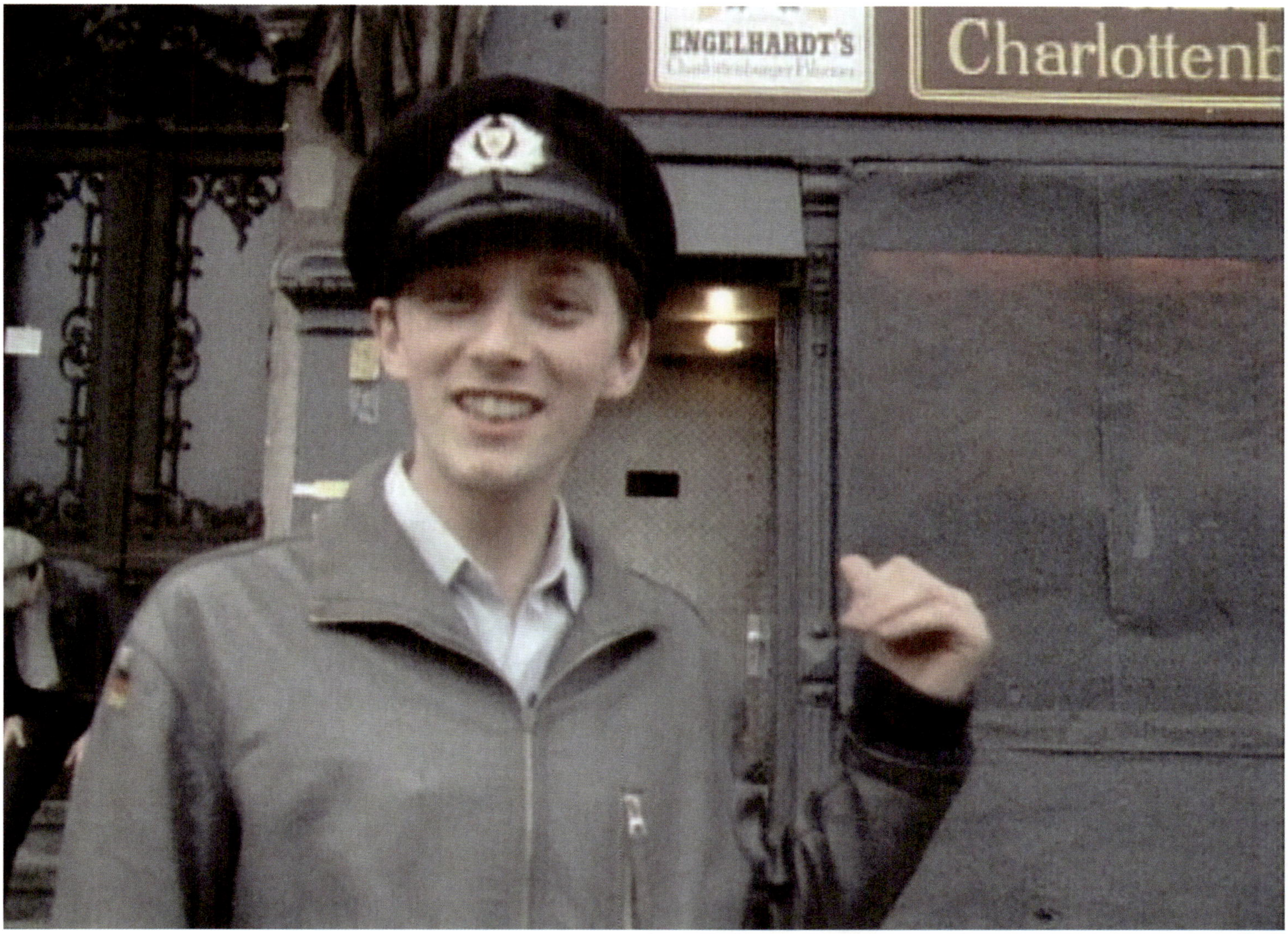
ENGELHARDT'S
Charlottenb

ausstrahlte. So konnte ich nach ein paar Stunden Fahrt wenigstens auf Deutsch bis zehn zählen, auch wenn mir die Reihenfolge vorerst ein Rätsel blieb.

Als wir endlich den Grenzübergang nach West-Berlin erreichten, kam ich mir vor wie in einem Science-Fiction- oder einem billigen Agentenfilm. Oh, my goodness — härtere Kontrollen hatte ich noch nie erlebt. Erst auf Aufforderung durfte man bis zur Haltelinie vorfahren. Mit einem einschüchternden Blick prüfte der Vopo sodann das Bild in meinem Pass und sah wiederholt zu mir rüber, um sich zu vergewissern, ob ich auch der war, dessen Pass er in Händen hielt. Doch im Gegensatz zu anderen Berlin-Reisenden, die aus der Schlange gewunken wurden und deren Auto von oben bis unten untersucht wurde, ob sich darin westliche Zeitungen befanden oder gar ein Flüchtling unter der Sitzbank versteckt hielt, hatte ich Glück: Der grimmig dreinblickende Grenzwächter ließ mich passieren und nach West-Berlin einreisen.

Die Stadt war überhaupt nicht so, wie ich sie mir vorgestellt hatte. Sie war viel aufregender und an jeder Ecke war etwas los. Berlin zeigte sich mir von seiner besten Seite. Obwohl ich sie nicht verstehen konnte, wurde ich von den Berlinern sehr freundlich begrüßt. Gleich am nächsten Tag hatte ich eine bezeichnende Begegnung mit einem Berliner. Ich wollte meine Eltern anrufen und benötigte Kleingeld zum Telefonieren. Also ging ich in eine typische Berliner Eckkneipe am Ende der Winterfeldtstraße. Eine Frau kauerte in gebückter Haltung hinter dem Tresen und räumte Flaschen ein, und ich fragte sie höflich in meinem besten Deutsch: „Entschuldigen Sie bitte, sprechen Sie Englisch?" Woraufhin sich ein zwei Meter großer Transvestit in vollem Horror-Make-up aufrichtete und umdrehte: „Ja, Schätzchen, wat willste?" Da wurde mir knallhart klar, dass ich in Berlin und gut aufgehoben war. In gewisser Hinsicht war Berlin noch abgefuckter als Manchester. An manchen Stellen sah es immer noch so aus wie im Mai 1945. Die grauen Häuser wiesen noch verstreut Schusslöcher vom Kampf mit den Russen auf. Wow! Es war faszinierend. Überall konnte man die Geschichte spüren. Die Stadt hatte etwas Klaustrophobisches an

that allowed me to travel all over Europe, so I embarked upon a tour across West Germany. Experiencing along the way impressive new looking cities such as Düsseldorf, Cologne, Frankfurt, Munich and Hamburg. Düsseldorf was interesting, and so was Hamburg, but Berlin had a different, magical attraction.

First, to get there I had to cross through the red sea of communist East Germany. Because I had missed my train connection, I decided to hitch-hike. I waited a mere 2 minutes at the West-East border, before a student picked me up. My credentials were carefully checked and I paid my exit fee of five west German – *Deutsch* - Marks for a transit visa. The ride made communist GDR - The German Democratic Republic - appear enormous, at least the monotonous hours trundeling along the unlit and bumpy transit road at 100 km per hour made it seem endless and from what I could see through the drizzling rain, it also looked pretty dreary too. This painful ride gave bump and grind a whole new meaning. Pure torture. Back then, I didn't speak a word of German, apart from things that I had learnt from warfilms. Useful phrases like "Hände hoch!" or "Achtung!", words which could surely have led to some misunderstandings if I wanted to buy some bread rolls. To complete the racket, the radio spewed out unfathomable coded numbers, a non-stop broadcast from the allies, probably for spies in the field. After a few hours of mind numbing numerical repetition, I could count to ten in German, although I probably couldn't have told you what order the numbers were in.

When we finally reached the border crossing to West Berlin, I felt like I was in a second hand spy film. Oh, my goodness: I had never experienced such a rigorous border inspection and it was seriously scary. Would they even let us out? You were allowed to slowly drive up to the designated stop line, and could only cross it after receiving permission from a surly border guard. With an intimidating glance, he closely examined the picture in my passport in order to make sure that I was the person whose passport he held in his hands. Thankfully, in contrast to the other poor devils travelling to West Berlin who were ordered out of the line and whose cars were searched from top to

sich und war irgendwie surreal. Ein schroffer, kalter Ort mit einer unglaublich intensiven Atmosphäre, der nach Kohleöfen roch.

Auf dem Kudamm saß jeden Tag eine seltsam anmutende ältere Frau, Helga Götze, vor der Gedächtniskirche, trug Gedichte vor und häkelte Deckchen mit Aufschriften wie „Ficken macht Spaß" oder „Wichs dir einen!" Es gab Roller-Discos und -Restaurants, in denen man von Transvestiten auf Rollschuhen bedient wurde. Damals hatten die Mädchen noch Schamhaare und die Jungs trugen Minipli-Dauerwellen, Herrenhandtaschen und Schnauzbärte und manche sogar Make-up. In den Kneipen und im Fernsehen rauchten die Leute wie Schornsteine, und nahezu jeder besaß einen Plattenspieler, einen Cassettenrecorder oder einen Walkman. Es gab besetzte Häuser, die Rote Armee Fraktion und den Paragraphen 175, der Homosexualität unter Strafe stellte. Vor Telefonzellen bildeten sich Schlangen, weil kaum jemand ein eigenes Telefon hatte, es gab Polaroid-Fotos und Super-8-Filme. Die D-Mark und natürlich die Mauer, die quer durch die Stadt verlief und sie in Ost- und West-Berlin teilte.

Es heißt, dass man nicht dabeigewesen sei, wenn man sich noch an die Achtzigerjahre erinnern könne. Doch ich war mittendrin im Geschehen und kann mich noch sehr gut daran erinnern. Zumindest hoffe ich das.

Gleich an einem der ersten Abende wollte ich Edgar Froese von Tangerine Dream besuchen, der auch für David Bowie ein wichtiger Kontakt in Berlin gewesen war; Bowie hatte bei ihm gewohnt, als seine Wohnung in der Schöneberger Hauptstraße 155 renoviert wurde. Als ich in der Sächsischen Straße klingelte, war ich total nervös. Seine Frau Monika öffnete mir mit einem Kind auf dem Arm die Tür — und musste lachen. Denn Edgar war nicht zu Hause, sondern gerade in England. Wie peinlich! Ich habe ihn dann erst 20 Jahre später kennengelernt.

Frustriert zog ich ab und begab mich erst einmal auf Spurensuche. Ich wollte die Läden sehen, in denen sich Bowie und Iggy Pop rumgetrieben hatten: das Schwulencafé Anderes Ufer in der Schöneberger Hauptstraße oder den Nachtclub Chez Romy Haag, in dem der Travestie-Star Zazie de Paris auftrat. Die Leute, die Bowie Ende der

bottom for weapons, ammunition or a possible escapee hiding under the back seat, we were lucky: the grim looking border guard even let us pass. We were through and finally free to enter into West Berlin and towards its alluring bright lights.

The city wasn't anything like I had imagined. It was much brighter and more alive. It appeared like on every street corner something was happening. Although I couldn't really understand them, the Berliners greeted me warmly. The next day after my arrival, I had my first encounter with a local.

I wanted to call my parents, but needed some small change to make the telephone call. I found a typical Berlin pub at the end of my street in Winterfeldtstrasse. The place was almost empty apart from a few old men sipping schnapps. A woman in a yellow polka-dot top was stooped over behind the bar, stocking away some bottles, and I asked her politely in my best German, "Excuse me please, do you speak English?" At this, the woman stood up and slowly turned around to reveal she was a six foot tall transvestite, with bright red hair and complete horror-show make-up, "Yesss, dahling", she hissed "what do you want?" WOW! It was immediately clear to me this was normal and every day here. Yes, I realised I was finally in Berlin - and in very good hands.

In a way, Berlin was more fucked up than Manchester. In some places, it still looked like it had back in May 1945 and I loved it. The grey and blackened battle scarred buildings still had bullet holes from the end of the war. It was utterly fascinating. One could sense history everywhere. The city had a bit of a claustrophobic feel to it and was somehow surreal, especially the eastern part, which felt almost like being beamed down into a sci-fi film. In winter, it became a rough, cold place with an unbelievably intense atmosphere, with the stench of burning coal from the ovens which were used to heat the houses.

I immediately felt at home. Berlin seemed full of weirdos. For example, every day on Kurfuerstendamm, an odd-looking elderly woman, Helga Götze, sat in front of the bombed out Kaiser Wilhelm Memorial Church, reciting erotic poetry and crocheting doilies with little epigrams

Siebzigerjahre in Berlin kennenlernte, die Modeschöpferin Claudia Skoda, den Travestie-Star Romy Haag oder den Maler Martin Kippenberger, waren fast alle Bohèmiens, wie es sie in Manchester nicht gab.

West-Berlin hatte schon damals keine Sperrstunde und nachts begegneten einem viele schräge Vögel, die in die Mauerstadt gekommen waren, um dem Wehrdienst in Westdeutschland zu entgehen oder der Enge ihrer Heimatstädte zu entfliehen. Die Verständigung mit Hippies, Punks und Hausbesetzern, Schwulen und Lesben gefiel mir, und ich lernte schnell neue Wörter wie „Kaputtniks" und „Radikalinski". Oder „geil" — eins der wichtigsten Adjektive überhaupt.

Nach dem Zweiten Weltkrieg war Berlin unter den vier Siegermächten aufgeteilt worden. Es gab einen amerikanischen, einen britischen und einen französischen Sektor, die vom russischen Sektor, Ost-Berlin, durch eine 45 Kilometer lange Mauer getrennt waren, die an den meisten Stellen dreieinhalb Meter hoch war und deren Fundament ein Meter unter der Erde lag, damit niemand darunter hindurchschlüpfen konnte. Der halbe Meter vor der Mauer gehörte offiziell zu Ost-Berlin, konnte aber vom Westen aus problemlos von Künstlern wie Thierry Noir oder Kiddy Citny betreten werden, um die Mauer zu bemalen, oder sie zu entflammen, wie es Kain Karawahn tat; Mitte der Achtzigerjahre engagierte der West-Berliner Senat sogar ausländische Künstler wie Keith Haring, um die dem Westen zugewandte Seite der Mauer zu verschönern. Wie für alle Touristen endete auch meine erste Sightseeing-Tour an der Mauer, die mit Parolen verziert war. „Zerstöre, was du nicht verstehst", lautete eine. „Wir alle brauchen das Licht zum Leben" eine andere. Oder es hieß einfach nur: „Eigentum der Klasse 10b". Als ich die Inschrift „MUFC" entdeckte, die Abkürzung von Manchester United Football Club, kam ich mir wie zu Hause vor.

Eine Wohnung zu finden, war kein Problem. Damals standen viele Häuser, die abgerissen werden sollten, leer. Der Student, der mich beim Trampen mitgenommen hatte, wohnte in einem solchen Haus in der Nähe des Nollendorfplatzes und bot mir an, ebenfalls dort einzuziehen. Ich war begeistert, denn dort hatte ich sechs

like "Fucking is fun" or "Have a wank". There were roller discos and roller restaurants where you would be served burgers by transvestites on rollerskates. Most girls back then didn't shave their pubic hair and boys sported tight-curled perms, carried male-handbags, wore big moustaches and some even make-up. In the pubs and on television, people smoked like chimneys and almost everyone had a record player, a cassette recorder, or a Walkman. There were squatted houses, the Red Army Faction and Paragraph 175 a law which criminalised homosexuality. People would queue up at the phone boxes because almost no one had their own telephone at home. We had Polaroid instant cameras and Super-8 films. We had the Deutsch Mark and of course, the Berlin Wall, which ran straight through the city, dividing communist East Berlin from capitalist West Berlin.

It is said that you if you can remember the 80's then you weren't there. But I was there, right in the middle of it and I can remember quite a lot. Well, at least I hope I can. On one of my first evenings, I struck up enough courage to go and visit Edgar Froese from Tangerine Dream. Edgar was an important contact for David Bowie in Berlin. Bowie had lived with him briefly while his apartment, on Hauptstraße in Schönebergs student district, was being renovated. As I pressed the door bell at Edgars flat on Sächsische Straße, I was so nervous. His wife, Monique, opened the door, holding a small child in her arms – and she had to laugh. Edgar wasn't at home but on tour in England. How embarassing! It took me 20 more years before I would finally get to meet him for the first time. Frustrated, I decided to go in search of all the clubs and bars where Iggy and Bowie had been, such as the predominantly gay café Anderes Ufer, a mere stone's throw away from Bowie's flat on Hauptstrasse, or the cabaret-esque nightclub Chez Romy Haag, where the delightful drag queen star Zazie de Paris performed. The people Bowie got to know while in Berlin at the end of the seventies, like the fashion designer Claudia Skoda, or drag queen Romy Haag and the artist Martin Kippenberger, were almost all a special type of bohemian, a species virtually non-existent in Manchester.

30/31: Mauerkunstaktionen
von Thierry Noir
▲ Keith Haring
▼ Kai Karawahn

Mal so viel Platz wie daheim in Manchester und sogar ein Marmorbad, Stuck an der Decke und einen Balkon. Und das auch noch in meiner Preisklasse — zum Nulltarif. Statt eines Schlüssels händigte man mir einen Dietrich aus. Viele Berliner Wohnungen waren spartanisch eingerichtete, fast möbelfreie Zonen mit vier Meter hohen Decken. Betten gab es nicht, nur Matratzen, die auf dem Boden lagen. Und weil man in einem besetzten Haus ständig befürchtete, dass die Wohnung von der Polizei geräumt wird, war man mobil und immer auf der „Flucht nach vorn", wie auch eine Band hieß.

Natürlich hatte diese Altbauwohnung in bester Lage auch kleine Makel. Draußen vor der Tür und in den Hinterhöfen steppte der Berliner Bär, und unsere Freunde und Helfer von der Polizei spielten mit uns Bürgerkrieg, bis uns von ihrem Gas die Tränen kamen. Die Staatsgewalt hatte unser Wohngebiet am Nolli zu ihrem Übungsplatz erklärt und jagte uns in ihren grünen Bullenwannen. Und wir jagten sie und bewarfen sie mit Pflastersteinen, weil wir so erfreut über ihren Einsatz waren.

Mit der Zeit wurde dieses Spiel ziemlich lästig. Doch es schreckte mich nicht ab, sondern trieb mich nur noch tiefer in diese Stadt hinein. Denn Berlin war zwar nicht schön, aber verdammt sexy.

One important factor for West Berlin's vibrant nightlife was that it didn't have a closing-time curfew, so at night you would meet quite a few weirdos who had fled to the walled city to avoid doing their obligatory military service in the West German Army, or to escape the suffocating narrow-mindedness of their home towns. The open minded tolerance and understanding between everyone in the city, hippies, punks and squatters, gay men and lesbians alike, really appealed to me, and I quickly learned new, unecessary words like "Kaputtniks" and "Radikalinski". Or "geil" — that was one of the most important German adjectives.

After World War II, Berlin was divided amongst the four allied powers. The American, British and French sectors were separated from the Russian sector - East Berlin - by a 45 kilometer long border wall that was, for most of its length, 3 meters high and with a foundation that lay another meter beneath the surface to prevent anyone from digging their way out to freedom. Actually, East Berlin officially began half a meter in front of the wall, although this didn't stop artists like Thierry Noir or Kiddy Citny from stepping up to it to daub paint on it, or to set it on fire, like Kain Karawahn did.

By the middle of the eighties, even the West Berlin Senate were clandestinely hiring foreign artists like Keith Haring to brighten up the West Berlin side of the wall.

Like most tourists, my first sightseeing tour also ended at the Berlin Wall, which was daubed with graffiti and aphorisms. Things like: "Destroy what you do not understand", "We all need light to live" or simply profanities like, "Property of class 10b". When I found the inscription "MUFC", which was the abbreviation for Manchester United Football Club, I really felt like I was back home again.

It wasn't that hard to find a flat to live in either. Many of the old houses were condemned to be torn down and most were just standing empty and abandoned. The student who had given me my ride to Berlin lived in one of these houses in Winterfeldstrasse close to Nollendorfplatz, and he offered me a place of my own, upstairs. I was thrilled, this huge flat had six times the space of my previous place, with a

marble bathroom, a stuccoed ceiling, parquet flooring and a balcony. And all for free, wich was well within my budget. Instead of a key, I was given a skeleton key.

Most Berlin flats tended to be rather spartan in their furnishings, they were essentially furniture-free zones with four-meter high ceilings. Most people had no beds, only mattresses on the floor. And since most squatters lived with the daily fear that the police would raid the flat and clear them out, everyone travelled light, ready to be able to leave at a moment's notice, and always prepared to venture forth.

Naturally, these wonderful old apartments, situated in the best of locations, weren't without their shortcomings. Although I had I had nice neighbours and extremely considerate flatmates, it seemed that directly in front of our door and out in the back courtyard danced the Berlin bear. By this time, the local council, suported by the police, were determinded to clear the houses of all unwanted elements. Our friend and helper played a game of civil war with us, until it literally drove us to tears. The authorities declared our living quarters to be their training area and they bashed us and gassed us and chased us down in their lumbering green police vans and we fought them back with cobble stones and molotov cocktails.

After a while, this game with the police became rather annoying and tiresome, but it didn't deter me, it just drove me deeper into the city's nightlife activities.

Arguably, Berlin wasn't beautiful, but it was damned sexy.

◀ Romy Haag
▲ Claudia Skoda

38-41: Georg-von-Rauch-Haus
42-43: Knut Hoffmeister
44-45: Kai Karawahn setzt die Mauer in Brand

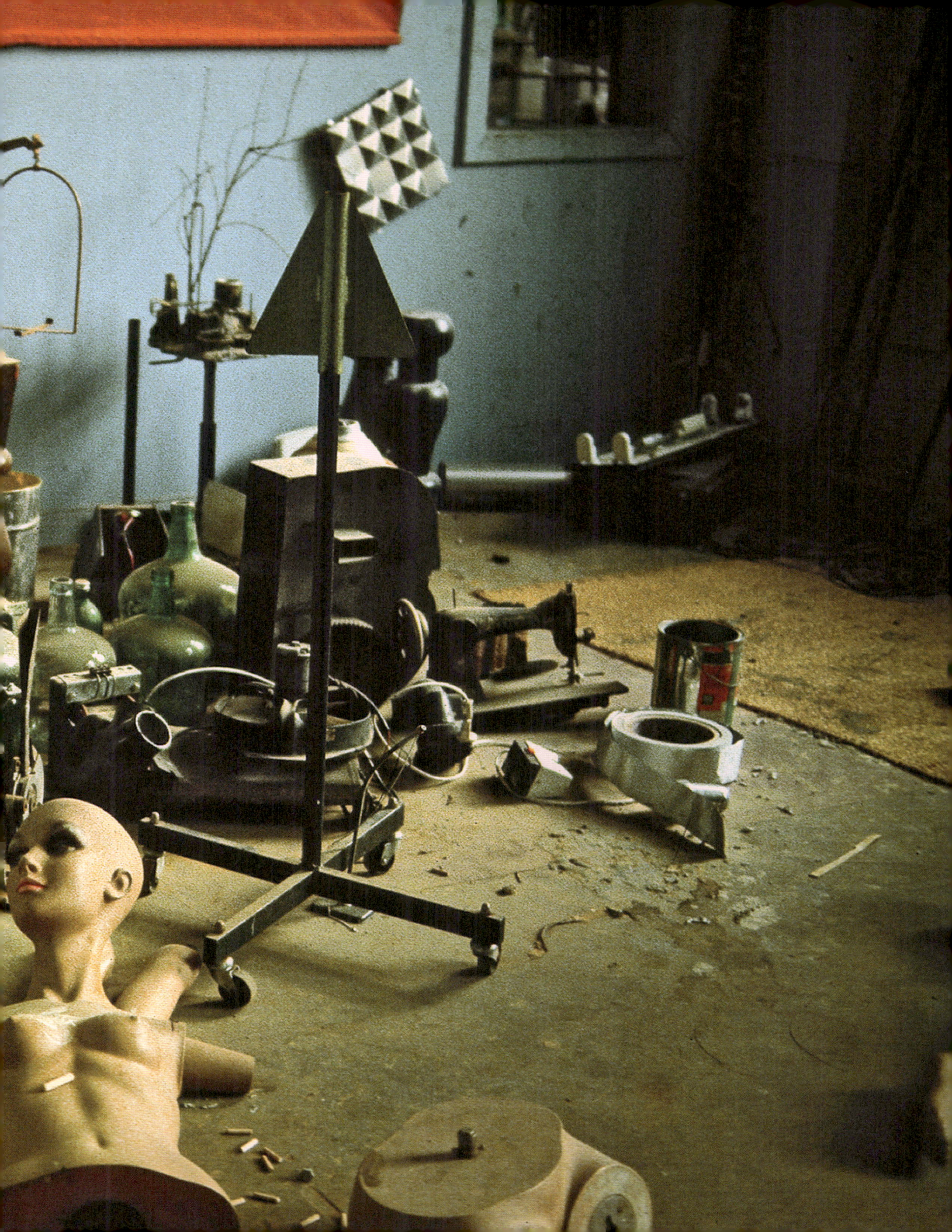

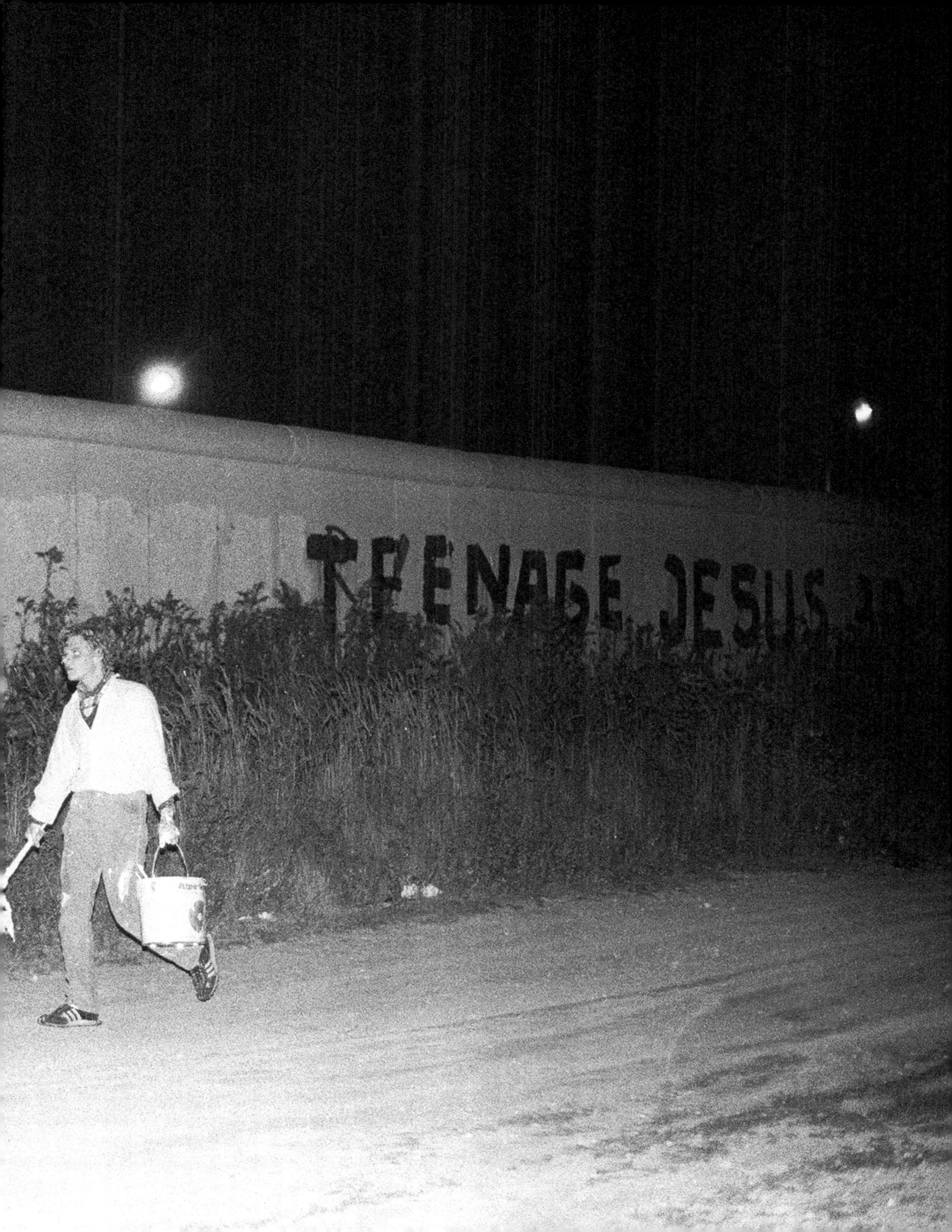
TEENAGE JESUS

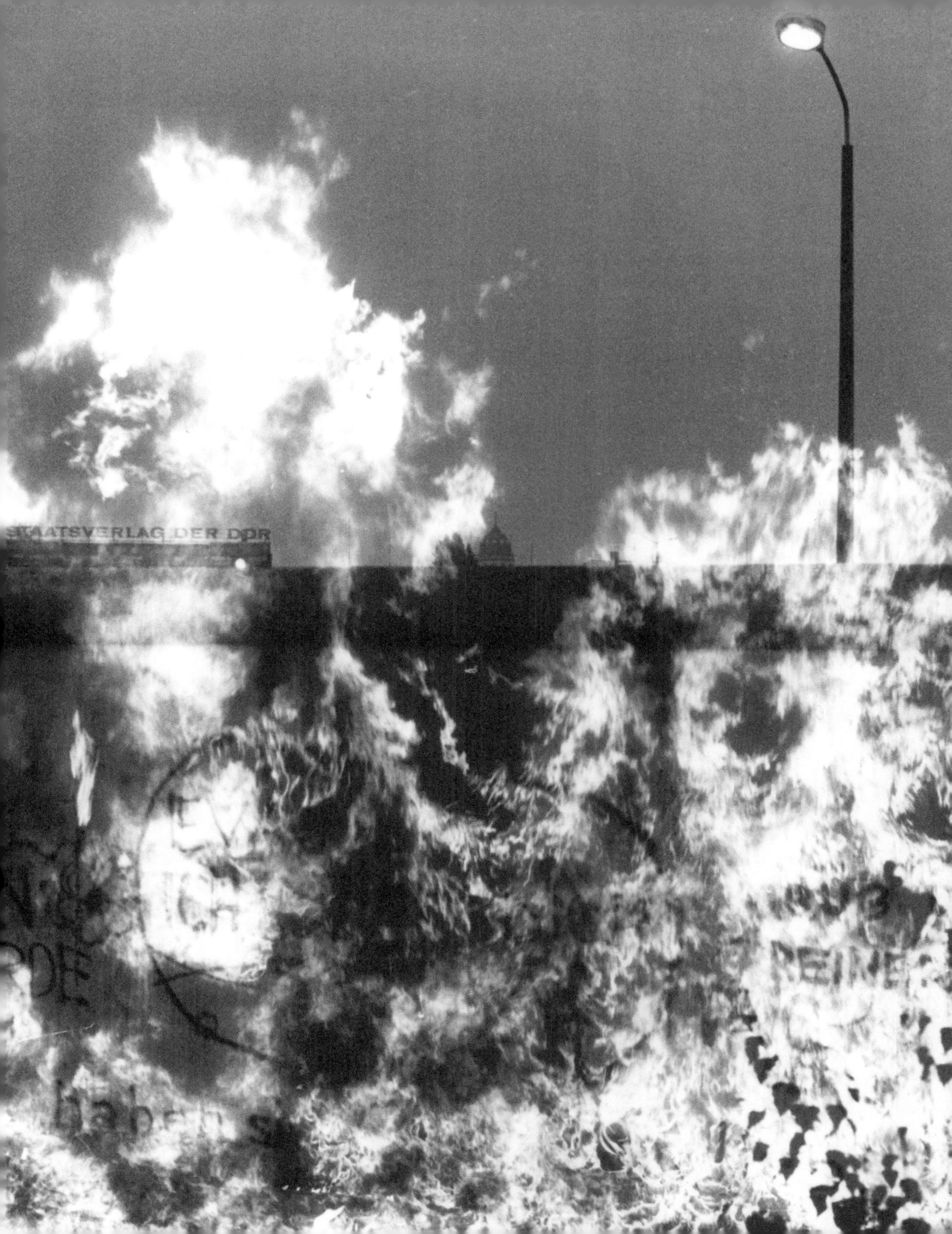

KOMA KINO

Dass ich nun in West-Berlin lebte, sprach sich in Manchester schnell herum. Ein alter Freund von mir, Rob Gretton, der Manager von Joy Division, schlug Tony Wilson, dem Fernsehmoderator, Gründer des neuen Indie-Labels Factory Records und späteren Mitbesitzer des Haçienda-Clubs, vor, mich mit der Promotion ihrer Platten in Deutschland zu betreuen, und so bekam ich schon bald kistenweise Platten von Bands wie Joy Division, Cabaret Voltaire, A Certain Ratio, Durutti Column oder Orchestral Manoeuvres In The Dark (OMD) geliefert, um sie an Radiosender und deutsche Musikzeitschriften wie BRAVO, Pop Rocky, Musik Express, Spex oder Sounds zu verschicken.

Die Resonanz war leider gleich null. Obwohl John Peels BFBS-Sendung in den Kreisen, in denen ich mich bewegte, Kult war und er fast religiös verehrt wurde, weil er „unsere" Platten spielte, interessierte sich fast niemand in Deutschland dafür. Allein Monika Dietl stellte sie im Zündfunk des Bayerischen Rundfunks vor.

Das lag vor allem daran, dass man in Deutschland gerade seine eigenen musikalischen Fähigkeiten wiederentdeckte und dabei war, eine eigene New Wave, die sogenannte Neue Deutsche Welle, zu kreieren. Da interessierte sich halt niemand für ein kleines Independent-Label aus Manchester und schon gar nicht für eine düster klingende Band wie Joy Division.

Im Januar 1980 half ich Factory Records, ein Konzert mit ihnen im Kant Kino zu organisieren, in dem auch schon Iggy Pop, The Vibrators, The Damned und Ultravox aufgetreten waren. Ich musste Rob Gretton geradezu anflehen, Berlin in den Tourneeplan aufzunehmen, und verschickte ihre neue Single „Transmission" an den RIAS und den SFB, doch sie wurde kein einziges Mal im Radio gespielt. Das war total frustrierend.

Factory Records legte viel Wert auf sein Image und das Design, und so war es mir fast peinlich, als ich das Plakat des Kant Kinos für das Joy-Division-Konzert sah. Es sah aus, als sei es von einem sechsjährigen Kind gemalt worden. Wie sollte ich das nur der Band erklären? Wenigstens wurde es nicht in der ganzen Stadt, sondern nur vor dem Kant Kino plakatiert. Vielleicht wurde das

Word soon got around Manchester that I was living in West Berlin. An old DJ friend of mine, Rob Gretton, the manager of Joy Division, suggested to Tony Wilson, the television presenter and founder of the recently formed indie label Factory Records (and the later co-owner of the Haçienda Club) that I should promote their records in Germany. First, I was only promoting the records from Joy Division, then later other Factory bands like Cabaret Voltaire, A Certain Ratio, Durutti Column, Crispy Ambulance and Orchestral Manoeuvres In The Dark (OMD). With great expectation, I would send the records of Manchesters finest bands to the radio stations and all the popular German music magazines like BRAVO, Pop Rocky, Musik Express, Spex or Sounds in the hope they would get played or reviewed.

Unfortunately, there was absolutely zero interest. Even though John Peels' BFBS and BBC World Service radio programmes were considered to be practically religious services within the circles I moved in and he was regarded as a holy figure simply because he played "our" records, sadly almost no one in Germany was interested in Joy Division. The only person I received any feedback from was Monika Dietl, who played their records a few times in her Zündfunk programme on Bavarian radio.

This was primarily due to Germany's recent rediscovery of its own musical identity, and its focus on creating its own version of punk, which would eventually become known as Neue Deutsche Welle (German New Wave). A sound probaby driven by the alluring success of such pop-punk drivel as Ca plane pour moi. As such, even though it was fashionable and well designed, no one cared a shit about a small independent label from Manchester and even less about a miserable sounding band like Joy Division.

Convinced that they probably had to be seen to be believed, I eventually persuaded Rob Gretton to bring Joy Division to Berlin and set about helping Factory Records to organise a concert with the band in the Kant Kino in January 1980. Kant Kino was the prestigious West Berlin venue where such greats as Iggy Pop, The

▶ Screenshot B-Movie

Konzert ja deshalb ein ziemlicher Flop. Es kamen nicht mal 150 Leute. Die Band konnte sich zudem nicht im Monitor hören, der Sound war grausig und der Gesang unverständlich, da ihr Sänger Ian Curtis live keine besonders kräftige Stimme hatte. Als sich jemand aus dem Publikum beschwerte, weil er die Texte nicht verstehen konnte, lagen die Nerven der Band bereits blank und ihr Gitarrist Bernard Sumner schleuderte ihm entgegen: „Speak fuckin English, you German *bastard*!" Danach war die Stimmung endgültig im Keller.

Ich hatte aber geahnt, dass Berlin Ian Curtis und Bernard Sumner trotzdem gefallen würde, und unternahm eine Sightseeing-Tour mit der Band. Ian, der sich damals bereits in einer persönlichen Krise befand, fühlte sich vor ihrer anstehenden US-Tournee wie ausgebrannt und suchte, wie David Bowie ein paar Jahre zuvor, in Berlin Abstand vom Business und kreativen Input. Er wollte unbedingt das Brandenburger Tor von der anderen Seite aus sehen, und er war beeindruckt von den Schusslöchern in den Hauswänden im Ostteil der Stadt, in die man einen Finger stecken konnte. Die hatten wir zuvor nur in Fernsehfilmen über Nazi-Deutschland und den Zweiten Weltkrieg gesehen.

Auf der Flexi-Disc „Komakino" verarbeiteten Joy Division kurz darauf ihre Eindrücke von Berlin. Es war eine ihrer letzten Aufnahmen. Vier Monate nach ihrem Auftritt im Kant Kino war Ian tot. Im Alter von gerade mal 23 Jahren hatte er sich erhängt. Für mich brach eine Welt zusammen.

Nach seinem Tod verkauften sich ihre Platten beim Zensor, einem Import-Plattenladen, der im Hinterraum der Modeboutique Blue Moon in der Belziger Straße in Schöneberg untergebracht war, aber stapelweise und ihre Single „Love Will Tear Us Apart" lief in jedem Berliner Club, der etwas auf sich hielt. Gudrun Gut, die damals beim Zensor arbeitete, ging dieser Szene-Hit allerdings schon bald auf den Geist, weil er ihr zu „hittig" war und alle nur noch ihn und nichts anderes kauften.

Ein paar Wochen vor Ians Tod hatte ich ihm vorgeschlagen, sich nach der US-Tournee eine Auszeit zu nehmen

Vibrators, The Damned and Ultravox had already played. I actually had to beg Rob Gretton to include Berlin in their tour schedule, but I was certain it would be good for Berlin and the band. I sent Joy Division's latest single *Transmission* to the local radio stations RIAS and SFB, but unfortunately, they only played it once on the radio. It was utterly frustrating.

Above all else, Factory Records valued its reputation and well designed image, and so I was really embarrassed when I saw the Kant Kino poster for the Joy Division concert. It was awful and looked like it had been drawn by a six year old child. After all my efforts, how could I explain this to the band? The only respite was that it wasn't plastered throughout the city, but only displayed in front of the Kant Kino itself. I will never know, but maybe the only ever Berlin concert by Joy Divison was a flop due to this glorious piece of advertising? Less than 150 people turned up for the show. For sure, the gig in itself was a total disaster too. Not only the sound was horrible, the band couldn't hear themselves in the monitors. They struggled through their set, but since their singer, Ian Curtis, didn't have a naturally strong voice, most of the songs were incomprehensible. So when someone from the audience shouted to turn the vocals up, their frustrated guitarist Bernard Sumner snarled back at him, "Speak fuckin' English, you German *bastard*!" The atmosphere took a bit of a stuka dive after that.

Regardless, I knew Ian Curtis and Bernard Sumner would really like Berlin, so I took the band on a sight-seeing tour of the city. Ian was entangled in the middle of a personal crisis, exactly like David Bowie was some years previously, when he sought distance and creative input in Berlin. Ian really wanted to see the Brandenburger Tor, especially from the East side and he and Bernard were very impressed with the bullet holes from the battle of Berlin, where they could actually stick their fingers in.

Shortly after, Joy Division recorded their impressions of Berlin on the free Factory flexi-Disc Komakino. It was to be one of their last recordings. Four months after appearing at Kant Kino, Ian was dead. At the tender age of 23 he

▶ Ian Curtis (Joy Division)

und nach Berlin zu kommen, doch daraus war nichts geworden. Als aus Joy Division nach seinem Ableben New Order wurde, nahm jedoch Bernard Sumner mein Angebot an, eine Zeit lang bei mir zu wohnen. Ich zeigte ihm einen neuen Dance-Club, das Metropol, in dem High-Energy-Disco-Musik aus den USA gespielt wurde, die ihn offenbar nachhaltig beeindruckte — die Musik von New Order wurde daraufhin jedenfalls ebenfalls elektronischer.

Als John Peel die erste Single der West-Berliner Mädchenband Malaria! in seiner Sendung auf BFBS vorstellte, wollte Bernard sie gerne mal kennenlernen. Nichts leichter als das — ich war ja ihr Manager!

had hanged himself. It was unbelievable. A whole world seemed to collapse before me.

After Ians death, there was a surge in the band's popularity and even their records were sold in Zensor, the shabby, but most essential import record store that was based in the back room of the fashionable clothes shop Blue Moon on Belziger Straße in Schöneberg. It was in this place that I had first met Gudrun Gut, who worked there. The last Joy Division single, "Love Will Tear Us Apart", was played in every club and bar. Gudrun claimed she didn't really like the success of this cult hit because it had become too popular, as everyone wanted to buy it and nothing else.

A few weeks before Ian's death, I had suggested that after their U.S. tour, he take some time off and come over to Berlin, but due to these unforseen circumstances that now wasn't going to happen. So, after Joy Division became New Order, Bernard Sumner took me up on my offer to come and stay with me for a while. In the hope of inspiring him to take his band in a new direction, I showed him one of my favourite dance clubs, The Metropol, the biggest gay disco in Europe, where deep, dark and trippy high energy disco music from the USA was played; I knew Bernard was a synthesizer fan and it certainly seemed to have made an impression on him, since the music from New Order thereafter became much more electronic, culminating in the magnificent Blue Monday.

When John Peel introduced the first single from the West Berlin all-girl band Malaria! on his program, Bernard really wanted to meet them. Nothing could have been easier – I was their manager!

▶▲ Mark Reeder mit Joy Division
in einem Berliner Hotel
und ▼ live mit Shark Vegas

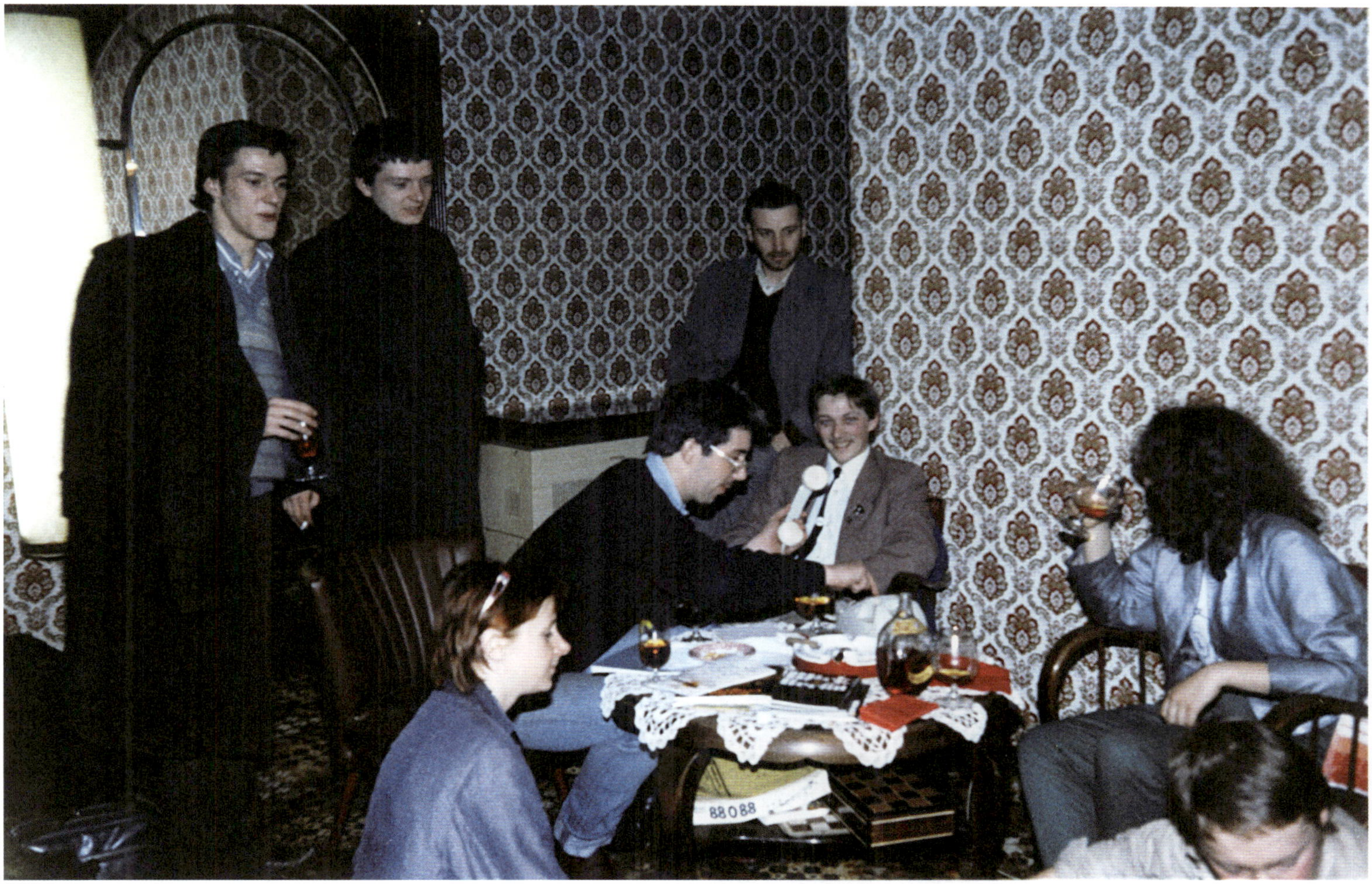
88088

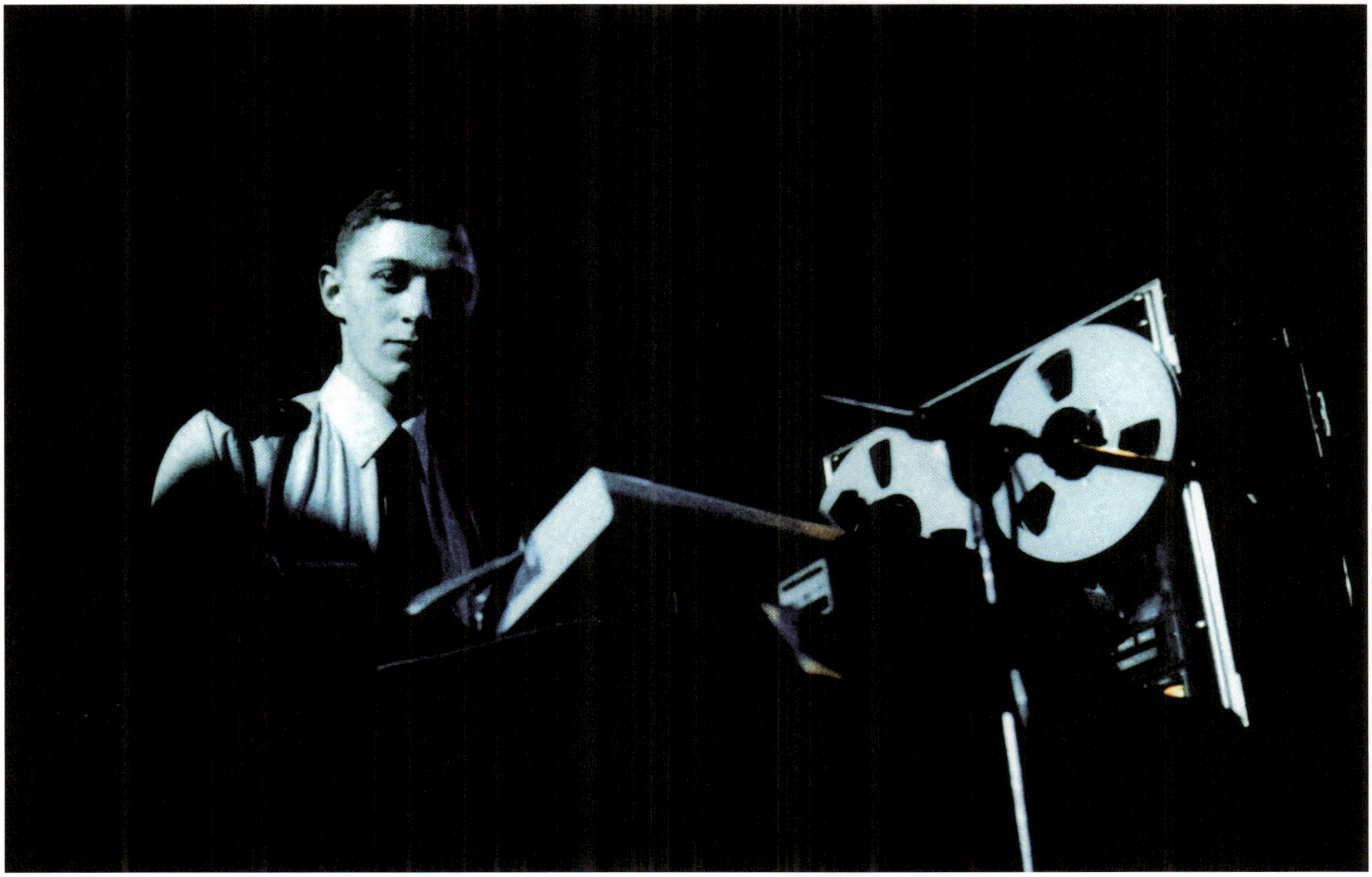

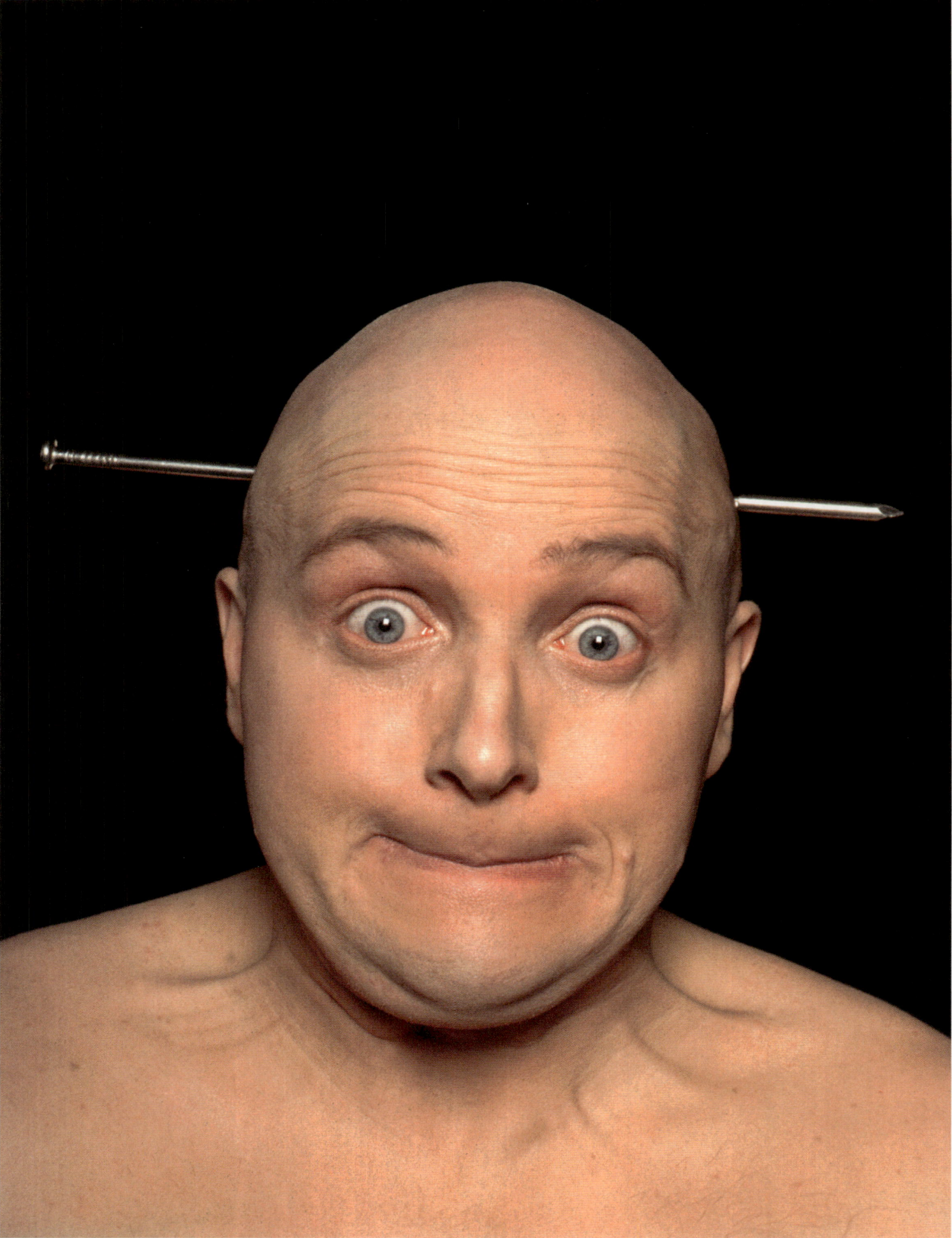

III
KALTES KLARES WASSER

Es lief einfach super. Ich war in Berlin, hatte ein Dach über dem Kopf und verdiente meinen Lebensunterhalt mit Musik. Obwohl ich kaum Deutsch sprach, bekam ich mit, wo die wildesten Bands spielten — im SO 36, einem schwer angesagten Punk-Club in Kreuzberg, in Laufweite zur Mauer. Dort lernte ich meinen Landsmann und künftigen Partner Alistair Gray kennen, als ich ihm bei einem Konzert auf den Fuß trat. Ein paar Monate später gründete ich gemeinsam mit ihm Die Unbekannten. Obwohl er noch nie in einer Band gespielt hatte, wurde er unser Sänger und Bassist.

Das SO 36 schien mir der perfekte Club für ein Konzert von New Order zu sein, und damit das Plakat diesmal auch ihrem Image entsprach, entwarf ich es lieber selbst, statt die Gestaltung dem Veranstalter Michael Voigt zu überlassen. Der Text darauf wurde allerdings von einem Drucker gesetzt, sodass ich ein weiteres Mal schockiert war: Bei der Unterzeile „New Order were Joy Division" hatte er ein „i" vergessen. Aber vielleicht ist das ja der Grund dafür, dass das Poster heute so höllisch hoch gehandelt wird.

Im SO 36 spürte man jedenfalls förmlich, wie hart am Rand sich die Künstler nicht nur mit ihrer Musik, sondern mit ihrer gesamten Existenz bewegten. In dem von Neonröhren erleuchteten Club gab es keine Flaschen, nur Dosen, und mit denen wurden schon mal die Bands beworfen, wenn sie dem Publikum nicht gefielen. Das gehörte irgendwie dazu. Und damit rechnete wohl auch jede Band, die dort auftrat. Nachdem ein Hagel von Bierdosen auf eine Punk-Band niedergegangen war, beschwerte sich ihr Sänger sogar: „Wat iss denn los? Habt ihr keene Büchsen mehr?"

Beim Zensor hatte ich Gudrun Gut kennengelernt. Sie war der Motor dieser neuen Musikszene und gründete ununterbrochen neue Bands. Nach einem Auftritt mit Mania D im Arsenal-Kino war ich total hin und weg gewesen, weil ihre Musik absolut dissonant und anders war als alles, was ich kannte. Und auch ihr nächstes Projekt, Malaria!, war eine Frauenband, wie man sie noch nie gesehen und gehört hatte.

Die Mädels grenzten sich von allem ab, vom Punk ebenso wie von der Neuen Welle, die gerade über Deutschland hereinschwappte. Sie wehrten sich vehement, in irgendeine

Everything was going quite smoothly. I was in Berlin, I had a roof over my head and was earning my living with music. Although I hardly spoke any German, I had ended up in a place where the wildest bands played – at the SO36 club, one of the best punk venues in Kreuzberg and only a short walking distance from the wall. There I met fellow Brit and my future partner, Alistair Gray, by stepping on his foot. A few months later, for the 17 June *Konzert zur Einheit der Nation,* we formed the band, *Die Unbekannten*. Although Alistair had never played in a band before, he became our singer and bass guitarist. Needless to say, our first gig was a total shambles, but apparently everyone thought we were very cool and avant-garde.

SO36 seemed to me to be the perfect place for the first Berlin gig by New Order. This time I wanted the poster to look good and correspond more to their image. So I decided to design it myself, instead of leaving it to the concert promoter Michael Voigt. I would create the text and image, but the type, would have to be set by the printer. When I received a copy of the finished poster I was in shock. The headline should have stated: "New Order were Joy Divsion" but unfortunately, the typesetter had omitted a letter "I" and it read instead, New Order were Joy Divsion. Perhaps this is the reason why this poster sells for such high prices nowadays? At the SO36 club, you could really feel how some of the performers lived on the edge, not only with their music but with their entire being. This club sold their drinks in cans, not bottles, which would usually end up being thrown at the musicians on stage if the crowd didn't like their music. That was part of the SO36 scene, and every band that got up on stage took that for granted. Once, after a hail of beer cans had stopped raining down on a punk band, the singer cheekily complained saying, "Whats up? Don't you have any more cans left?"

I had got to know Gudrun Gut at Zensor and I had meanwhile discovered she was the main driving force behind this new music scene. She was continuously starting up new bands. After a gig with Mania D at the Arsenal Kino, I was blown away because their music was so refreshing and unconventional, it was pure dissonance and so different from everything I knew. Gudrun's next project, Malaria!,

◀ Gudrun Gut (links) und Bettina Köster von Malaria!

58–59: Malaria!

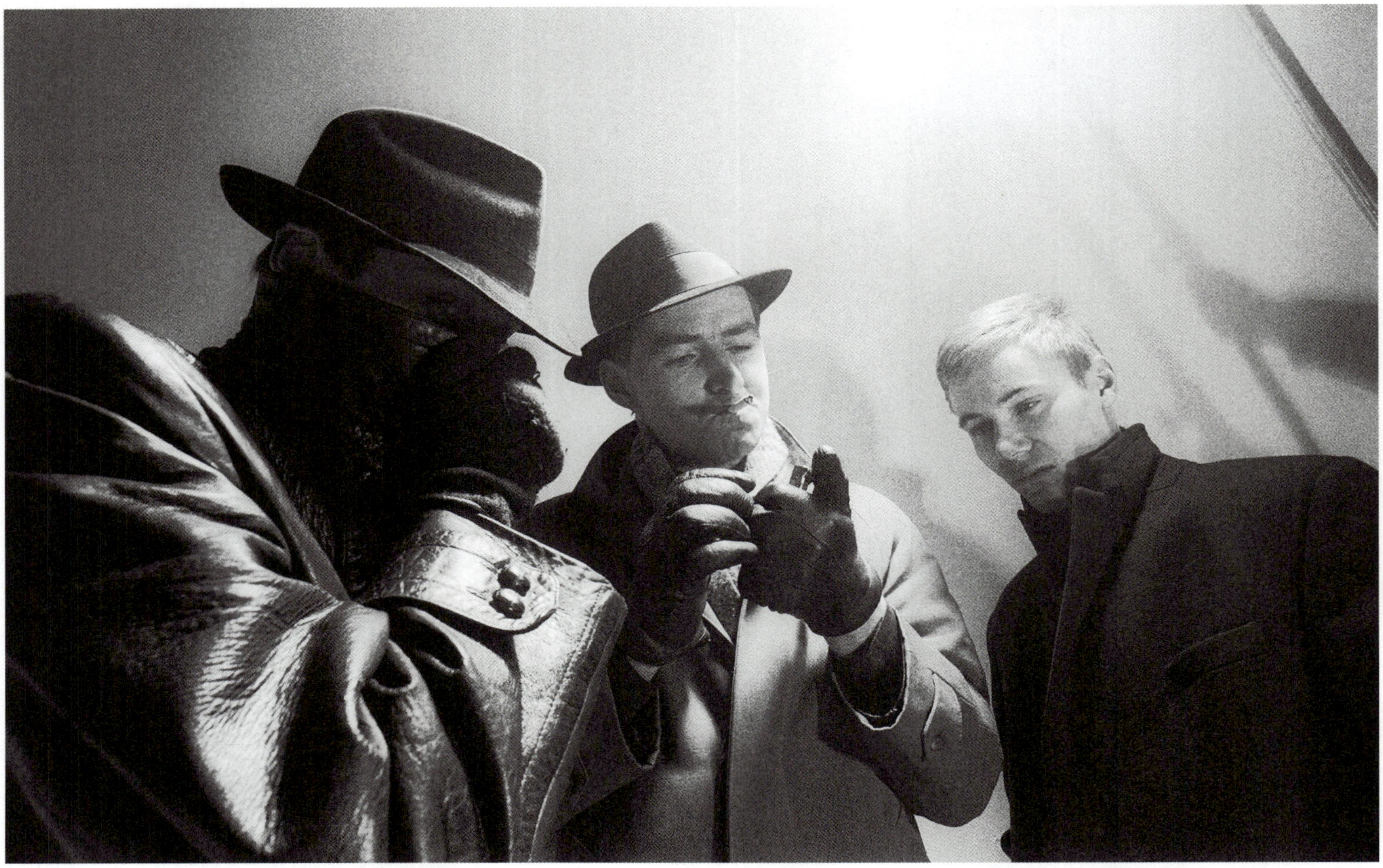

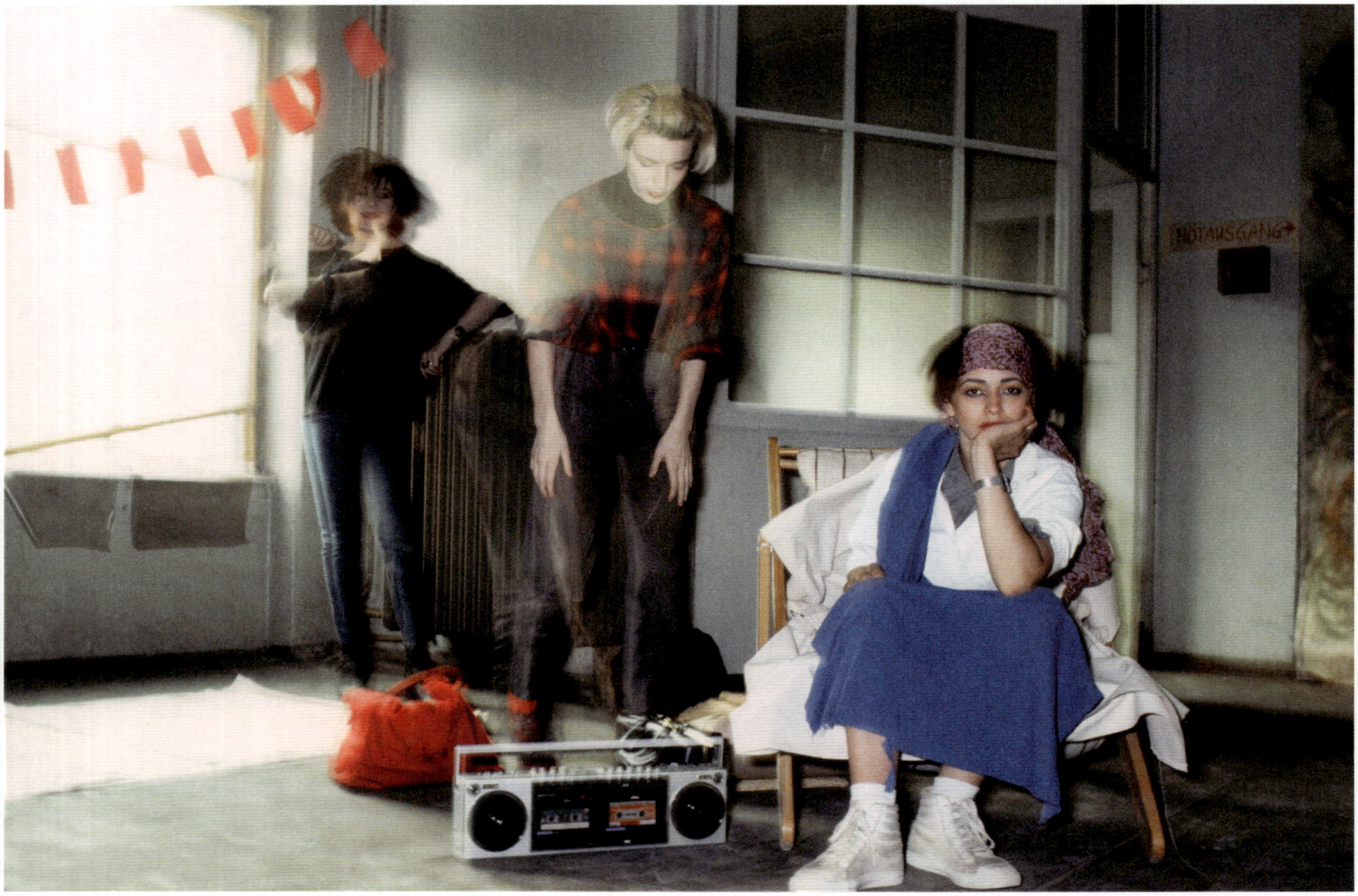
NOTAUSGANG

Schublade gesteckt oder mit anderen Bands verglichen zu werden: „Obwohl jetzt gerade Joy Division so in Mode sind, spielen wir trotzdem nicht wie Joy Division." Malaria! schrieben zudem sehr ungewöhnliche Texte zu Songs wie „How Do You Like My New Dog?", „Geh duschen" oder „Kaltes klares Wasser": „Über meine Hände, über meine Arme, über meine Schultern, über meine Beine, über meine Schenkel, über meine Brust, ich lasse meine Augen zu … kaltes klares Wasser."

Gudrun Gut und Bettina Köster, die Sängerin und Saxophonistin der Band, wollten, dass ich sie manage. Schließlich war ich Engländer und kannte mich sowohl musikalisch als auch in der noch kleinen Szene aus. Vor allem aber mochte ich auch ihre Musik. Sie versprachen sich davon wohl, dass es ihr Verdienst wäre, wenn alles gut, und ich Schuld hätte, wenn alles schief liefe. Und sie erzählten jedem, ob der es wissen wollte oder nicht: „Mark Reeder ist unser Manager." Mir selbst war das eher peinlich, weil es so kapitalistisch klang. Ich mochte die Beiden und fand die Band großartig. Aber eigentlich war ich doch nur ihr Roadie und Mixer, ihr Booker und ihr Männchen für alles.

Wie auch immer — Malaria! waren echt anders: androgyn, geheimnisvoll und vor allem sehr schräg. Diese Mädchen machten eine härtere Musik als die meisten Männer, und sie wirkte auch auf die Leute ziemlich brutal, die zu ihren Konzerten kamen, weil sie eben Mädchen waren, die mit ihrer Musik aber oft nichts anfangen konnten. Sie brachen alle Rock'n'Roll-Regeln, die ich aus England kannte, und das fand ich großartig. Anfangs powerten Malaria! einfach drauflos und fabrizierten total dilettantisch Krach. Nachdem sie eine Live-Aufnahme von sich angehört hatten, entwickelten sie aber einen speziellen Sound, und Gudrun Gut verkündete selbstbewusst: „Es macht viel mehr Spaß, mit Mädchen zu arbeiten als mit Jungs. Jungs wollen dir immer erzählen, was richtig und was falsch ist." Da war ich wohl eine Ausnahme, denn mir vertrauten sie.

Als Malaria! auf einem lesbischen Festival am Funkturm auftraten, wollte ich mich nach dem Soundcheck über das gigantische und lecker aussehende Buffet hermachen, das für alle beteiligten Musikerinnen angerichtet worden war.

was also an all girl band, but quite unlike anything anyone had seen or heard before.

The girls distanced themselves from everything that had gone before them, from punk as well as the German New Wave that was currently flooding over Germany. They vehemently resisted any sort of effort to pigeonhole them or compare them to other bands. Gudrun was adamant "Although Joy Division are really popular right now, we don't want to sound like Joy Division." Malaria! also wrote rather unconventional lyrics to their songs too, like "How Do You Like My New Dog?", or they courted controversy with "Geh Duschen" or "Kaltes Klares Wasser".

Gudrun Gut and Bettina Köster, the lead singer and saxophone player of the band, wanted me to manage their band. Not only was I English, but I understood their music and I knew my way around the still emerging new music scene. They probably convinced themselves that if everything went well, they had earned it, and if it failed, it would be my fault. They told everyone, whether they wanted to know it or not, "Mark Reeder is our manager." This was incredibly embarrassing for me because it sounded so capitalist, but I liked them both though and I thought their band was brilliant. Yet in reality, I was only their roadie, their support act, their sound engineer, their booking agent and ultimately their gofer.

In any event, Malaria! were really different: androgynous, mysterious, and most of all, really bizarre. These girls played music that was harder than most boys, and they came across as pretty brutal to most people who came to their concerts, not only because they were girls, but people didn't know how to categorise or evaluate their kind of music. They broke all the rules of Rock'n'Roll that I knew from England - and I thought that was brilliant. In the beginning, Malaria! just appeared to bash about and make a dilettantic noise, but after they heard themselves from a live performance, they started to develop a very special sound. Gudrun Gut said frankly: "It's much more fun to work with girls than with guys. Guys are always trying to tell you what's right and what's wrong." I guess I was one of the exceptions, since I was someone she trusted.

However, things with the girls weren't always quite so easy.

▲ Die Unbekannten
▼ Matador

Bevor ich auch nur einen Happen essen konnte, wurde ich jedoch ziemlich ruppig gefragt, ob ich endlich fertig sei — und von zwei recht großen Frauen unter den Armen gepackt und rausgetragen, ohne dass meine Füße den Boden berührten! Hilflos protestierte ich, ich hätte noch nichts gegessen, doch die Beiden kannten keine Gnade: „Du willst was essen? ...Moment ...‟ Eine von ihnen schmiss mir einen Zehnmarkschein vor die Füße und meinte nur: „Da drüben ist 'ne Pizzeria.‟

„Aber was ist mit heute Abend? Ich muss doch Malaria! mixen ...‟

Barsch entgegnete sie: „Heute Abend gibt es keinen Mann hier, nur Frauen.‟

Ich spielte kurz mit der Idee, mich als Frau zu verkleiden und mir ein Bärtchen anzumalen, wie ich es bei einigen Konzertbesucherinnen gesehen hatte, doch Malaria! mussten an diesem Abend ohne mich auskommen. Den Mädels zufolge soll ihr Sound katastrophal gewesen sein. Aber nicht nur dort war der Sound ein Problem. In Florenz spielten sie ein paar Monate später auf der Piazza vor mehreren Tausend Leuten. Dieser Open-Air-Auftritt war für mich der pure Horror und der Sound stürzte mit einem mega-lauten „Whummpf‟ ab, als Bettina in einem Wutanfall elfmeterreif gegen die DI-Box trat, die in der Mitte der Bühne postiert war.

Die „Queens of Noise‟ (John Peel) traten zusammen mit Nina Hagen im New Yorker Studio 54, im dortigen Mudd Club und in der Danceteria auf und gingen auch mit Birthday Party auf Tournee, einer australischen Band um den Sänger Nick Cave. Da ich selbst eine Band gegründet hatte, Die Unbekannten, und ohnehin als ihr Mixer dabei war, bot es sich zudem an, beide Gruppen als Package zu verkaufen. So kam auch ich in den Genuss von Live-Auftritten.

Wie es sich damals gehörte, bemusterte ich auch den englischen Radio-DJ John Peel mit der ersten Malaria!-LP, dessen Stimme mir seit meiner Jugend vertraut war und den ich persönlich kennengelernt hatte, als er eine Sendung für den Sender Freies Berlin (SFB) produzierte und ich ihn in Ost-Berlin mit echten Ost-Berliner Fans zusammenbrachte. John Peel hatte bereits die Mania-D-

Malaria! were booked to perform at a lesbian festival at the Berlin Funkturm (Radio Tower). I had just completed their soundcheck and I was really looking forward to getting something to eat at the delicious buffet spread that had been laid out for the participating musicians. But before I could even get in a bite, I was asked by two rather butch looking ladies if I was finally finished – they then grabbed me under the arms and literally frog-marched me out! My feet didn't even touch the ground. I tried my best to explain that I hadn't eaten, but the two had absolutely no pity for me: "You want to eat something? … Wait …" One of them quickly threw a ten Mark note at my feet and said sharply, "There's a pizzeria over there." „But what about tonight? I'm supposed to be mixing the sound for Malaria!" Their brisk response was: "There are no men allowed in here tonight. Only women."

I briefly toyed with the idea of dressing up like a woman and drawing on a little fake beard, like I had seen on some of the audience, but in the end it was no use, Malaria! had to get along without me that evening. According to the girls, their sound was a catastrophe.

But that wasn't the only place where the sound was a bit of a problem. A few months later, Malaria! played in Florence on a piazza in front a few thousand people. This promising open-air performance became a real nightmare for me, especially when Bettina, in a fit of rage, peanalty kicked the D.I sound box located right in the middle of the stage. The entire sound system imploded with a massive loud "Whummpf".

Internationally, the "Queens of Noise" (as John Peel so lovingly called them) were always well received and they performed together with Nina Hagen at New York's Studio 54, and at the Mudd Club and at the Danceteria, they also went on tour with The Birthday Party, an Australian band fronted by their illustrious singer Nick Cave. Since I myself had also started up a band, Die Unbekannten and was their live sound mixer anyway, it always seemed the natural thing to offer both our groups together as a package. That was how I came to savour the pleasure of our live performances. Proudly, I sent BBC radio DJ John Peel a copy of the first Malaria! album. His voice was an important part of my youth

▶ Nina Hagen

Scheibe „track 4" zur „Single des Jahres" erklärt, offenbar war ihr Album *Emotion* aber nicht angekommen: John bedauerte, dass er es „leider noch nicht" hatte, und legte stattdessen einen Track von der „Hausfrauen"-Seite des Albums *New York — Berlin* auf.

Ende 1980 lernte ich Adrian Wright kennen, ein Mitglied von The Human League. Bettina Köster hatte ihn eingeladen, Weihnachten in Berlin zu verbringen. Er war kaum angekommen, da vertraute sie ihm auch schon die Schlüssel ihrer Wohnung an und meinte nur: „Schließ ab, wenn du ausgehst, ich fahre über Weihnachten zu meiner Mutter." Und damit er nicht so allein war in der fremden großen Stadt, gab sie ihm meine Telefonnummer. Völlig hilflos und verzweifelt, rief er mich an. Ich holte ihn ab, wir kochten zusammen, und Silvester gingen wir zur *Last Night of the Excess Club*, der letzten Veranstaltung in diesem Club, bevor er geschlossen wurde, weil sich darüber eine Seniorenresidenz befand, der dieser Club wohl zu laut und zu exzessiv war.

Weil ich für Factory Records arbeitete, hatte mir der Veranstalter Michael Voigt vorgeschlagen, an diesem Abend ebenfalls aufzutreten. Er brauchte einfach einen Lückenfüller. Daraus wurde dann ein sehr, sehr chaotischer Auftritt. Gemeinsam mit Adrian Wright und Thomas Wydler, der später bei Die Unbekannten, den Bad Seeds und Die Haut Schlagzeug spielte, standen wir um vier oder fünf Uhr morgens auf der Bühne. Hackedicht vom Scheitel bis zur Sohle, spielten wir ein paar Titelmelodien von James-Bond-Filmen und einen eigenen Song, den wir ein paar Minuten vor unserem Auftritt geschrieben hatten, und beschimpften zwischendurch das Publikum. Der Club hieß eben nicht umsonst Excess.

Das Berliner Nachtleben war ohnehin recht außergewöhnlich. Es fing nicht vor Mitternacht an und dauerte meistens bis neun Uhr morgens. Nicht so wie in England, wo spätestens nachts um zwei Uhr alles schon vorbei war. Die Oranienstraße war sozusagen die Hauptstraße von Kreuzberg, aber obwohl achtzig Prozent der Läden in türkischer Hand waren, trafen sich Schwule und Lesben und Heteros in der O-Bar und hingen dort ab, bis die „Zentrale des Versackens" (Heinrich Dubel) morgens

and he undoubtedly influenced my taste in music. I'd got to know him personally when he came to Berlin. He was thrilled when I brought him over to East Berlin to meet his real Eastie fans. He had already pronounced the Mania-D record "track 4" as his single of the year; but apparently their album *Emotion* hadn't arrived, so John regretfully claimed that he "unfortunately didn't have it yet" and therefore, was resigned to play a track from the "hausfrauen" side of Malaria!s mini-album *New York — Berlin* instead.

At the end of 1980, I was introduced to Adrian Wright, a member of the synth pop band, The Human League. Bettina Koester had invited him to spend Christmas and New Year's in Berlin. He had barely arrived, when she gave him her key and said briefly, "Lock up when you go out. I'm going to my mum's for Christmas" and just so that he wouldn't feel completely alone in this big, unknown city, she gave him my telephone number and told him to ring me. Completely helpless and desperate, he gave me a call. That night, we met up, drank and cooked together, and a week later on New Year's Eve, I arranged for us to go to the *Last Night of the Excess Club*, the final three-day event to be held in this club before it closed down - since it was located beneath a retirement home and the noise was apparently just too loud and extreme.

Most probably because I was working for Factory Records, the promoter Michael Voigt thought it would be a good idea if I also performed that night as well. In reality I guess he just needed a gap filler. However, this turned out to be a very, very chaotic gig. Together with Adrian Wright and Thomas Wydler, who later played drums with Die Unbekannten, Die Haut and the Bad Seeds, we finally fell on stage at about four or five in the morning. By this time we were completely shitfaced. I vaguely recall that we *played* a mixture of James Bond themes and one of our own compositions that we had written just a few moments before going on stage, cursing the audience in between. I guess the club wasn't called Excess for nothing.

Berlin nightlife was, it must be said, rather extraordinary. It wouldn't get started before midnight and lasted until at least nine in the morning. Nothing like in Britain where everything was over by one or two a.m at the latest.

▶ Thomas Wydler (links) und Mark Reeder von Die Unbekannten
66-67: Shark Vegas live im Loft
68-69: Performance in der Oranienbar

eine Stunde lang zum Saubermachen geschlossen wurde und ein neuer Tag begann.

Als ich nach Berlin gekommen war, hatte ich nicht gewusst, was mich eigenlich erwartete. Ich hatte gedacht, ich hätte meine Hausaufgaben gemacht, und Klaus Schulze und Tangerine Dream gehört, vor Ort lernte ich aber Alexander Hacke alias Alexander von Borsig und Michael Schäumer von P1/E kennen, die eine ganz andere Art elektronischer Musik machten, eher elektronischen Punk Rock. Meine Vorstellung von deutscher Elektronik war völlig veraltet. Das waren ganz andere Leute, mit denen ich nun zu tun hatte, und sie hatten völlig andere Ansichten. West-Berlin hatte ein ganz anderes Ambiente, und die Leute, die ich in den Clubs und Bars traf, waren nicht so drauf wie die, denen ich in Manchester begegnet war.

Zum Beispiel Gudrun Gut. Sie machte nicht nur mit Malaria! und vielen anderen Projekten Musik, sondern betrieb auch mit einer Freundin einen Klamottenladen in der Goltzstraße, wo sie selbstgestrickte und entworfene Kleider und Pullover verkauften. Das Eisengrau, so sein Name, wurde schnell zum Anziehungspunkt für die neue Berliner Musikszene und hatte einen Untermieter, der im Laden auf einer Matratze hauste — Blixa Bargeld. Blixa war einer der schrägsten Vögel Berlins und Gudruns bester Freund. Als seine Band, die Einstürzenden Neubauten, am 1. April 1980 zum ersten Mal auftrat und im Moon Musik zu Super-8-Filmen machte, gehörten auch Gudrun und Beate Bartels neben Blixa und Andrew Unruh zur Erstbesetzung. Nachdem sie gemeinsam ein paar Mal aufgetreten waren, ging es bereits ins Studio. Dort wurden sie sich aber nicht so recht einig und Gudrun erkannte, „dass das Blixas Projekt war, sein Ding", und stieg wieder aus.

Oranienstrasse was the main street of Kreuzberg, and although about eighty percent of the shops were Turkish-owned, everyone regardless of their orientation would would meet in the O-bar. If you landed here you usually stayed until this *hardcore dive* (Die Zentrale des Versackens - Heinrich Dubel) would close for an hour, to clean up … and the new day would start.

When I first arrived in Berlin, I really had no idea what to expect from the city's nightlife. I thought I had done my electronic music homework by listening to Klaus Schulze und Tangerine Dream – but I soon found out. After meeting Alexander Hacke *(a.k.a. Alexander von Borsig)* and Michael Schaeumer from P1/E, I discovered two people who made a entirely different style of electronic music, it was much more like Daniel Miller's TVOD. It was electronic punk rock. I was very excited to find that here. My idea of German electronic music it appeared, was completely outdated. These people had different ideas altogether. West Berlin was beginning to develop an otherworldly atmosphere, and the people that I met in the clubs and bars had a different outlook. They weren't as obsessed by commercial success like the people I'd previously met in Manchester.

Take for example, Gudrun Gut. She wasn't only playing music with Malaria! she was participating in many other projects too, she also ran a little clothes shop on Goltzstrasse with a friend, where they sold handmade and hand-designed dresses and jumpers. The Eisengrau (iron grey) was its name, and it soon became a hangout for the new Berlin music scene. This shop also had a lodger who slept on a old mattress in the back of the shop - Blixa Bargeld. Blixa was a little unorthodox, even by Berlin standards, but he was one of Gudruns best friends.

She performed with Blixa for the first time in his new band, Einstürzende Neubauten on April 1st 1980, to Super-8 films, with Beate Bartel and Andrew Unruh who were the first members of this band. After they had performed a few times together, they went into the recording studio. Unfortunately, things didn't work out and Gudrun soon realised that Neubauten was really his thing and decided to leave.

▲ Leuchtreklame des SO 36
▼ Alex Hacke aka Alexander von Borsig im Risiko

S.O.36

NECRO
AUS LAUTER LIEBE
SPRUNG DEN
AUS WOLKEN
U.K.SUBS
Nicht saufen
alle

◀ Alex Hacke
▶ Flucht nach vorn
74-75: Sprung aus den Wolken
76-77: Einstürzende Neubauten im SO 36

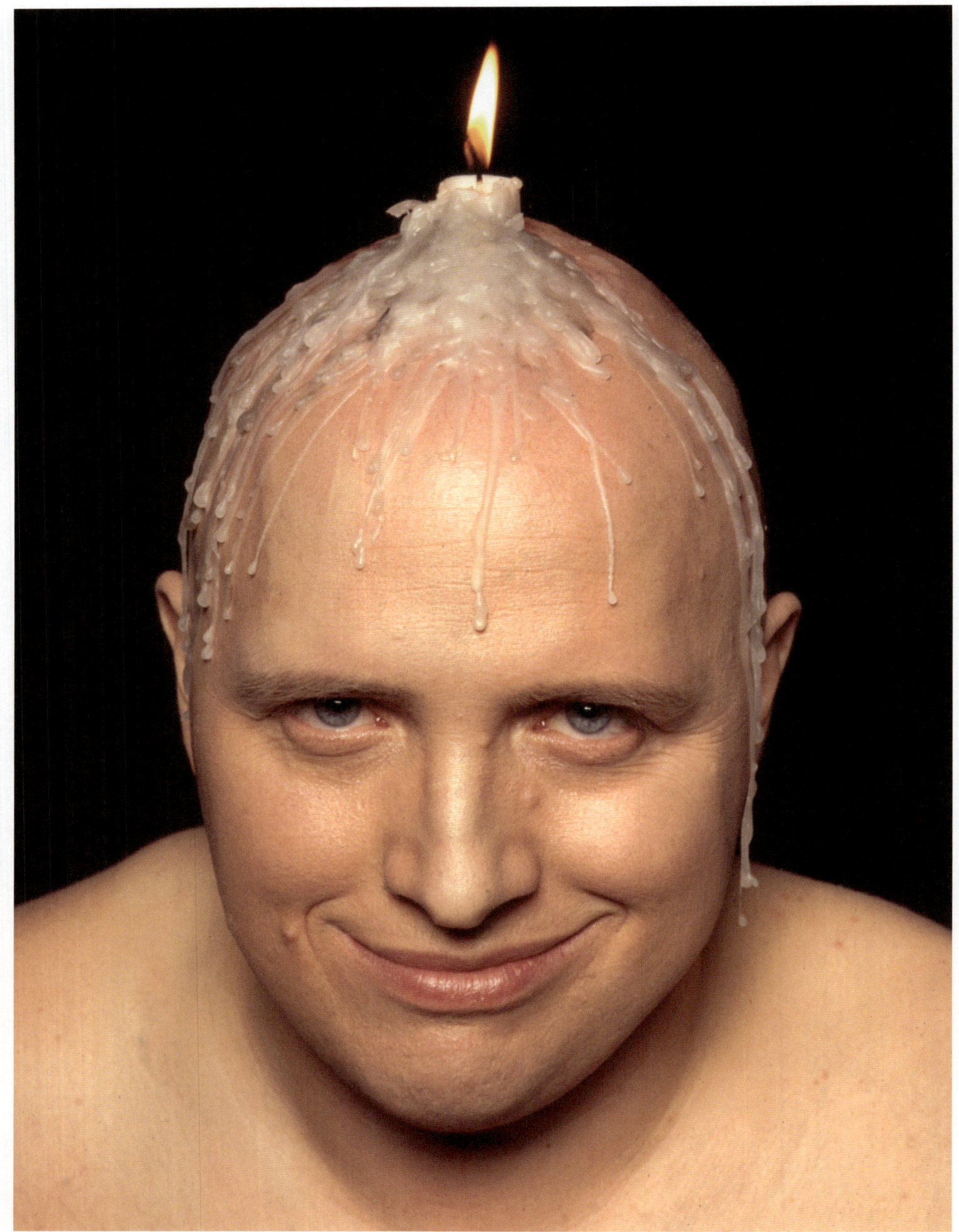

IV

KRIEG GEGEN DEN SCHLAF

THE WAR AGAINST SLEEP

Blixa Bargeld und seine Band, die er nach dem Einsturz der „schwangeren Auster", wie die Berliner Kongresshalle im Volksmund hieß, Einstürzende Neubauten genannt hatte, waren die Speerspitze einer neuen Generation von Musikern, die sich selbst als *Geniale Dilletanten* bezeichneten und den etablierten Musikbetrieb radikal ablehnten.

Blixa hatte keinen Schulabschluss, keinen Job und keine Wohnung, aber eine Band nach der anderen gegründet, bevor er Expeditionen in die Industriebrachen von West-Berlin unternahm und in einem vergessenen Hohlraum unter einer Autobahnbrücke anfing, Musik zu machen, ohne groß Instrumente oder Equipment zu besitzen. Für ihn hatte dieser Ort etwas Magisches, und er schwor auf seine „unglaubliche akustische Qualität".

Dieser Hohlraum war etwa vierzig Meter lang, aber gerade mal einen Meter fünfzig hoch, sodass er seine Gitarre in gebückter Haltung malträtieren musste, während Lastkraftwagen über ihn hinwegrauschten. Kein Wunder, dass es dort ziemlich schwierig für ihn war, Musik zu machen, die „was mit Friedensbewegung zu tun hat".

West-Berlin war für Blixa der „Nullpunkt", eine sehr seltsame, aber kreative Insel, die sich von allen anderen Städten unterschied. Die Mieten lagen weit unter dem Niveau der Bundesrepublik, man konnte mit einem Minimum an Geld überleben, und das lockte viele Typen aus Westdeutschland an, die nicht zur Bundeswehr wollten, aber auch alle möglichen Leute aus anderen Ländern, die sich daheim nicht entfalten konnten.

Als Brite gelangte ich relativ einfach an den Grenzübergängen Checkpoint Charlie oder Friedrichstraße nach Ost-Berlin. Ich musste nur ein Tagesvisum für fünf D-Mark kaufen und 25 D-Mark in nutzloses DDR-Monopolygeld pflichtumtauschen (von dem ich mir Propagandamaterial und Lenin- und Marx-Büsten kaufte). Ein West-Berliner musste hingegen erst ein Formular ausfüllen und drei Tage oder manchmal eine Woche lang warten, bis er ein Einreisevisum erhielt, und sich dann einer beängstigenden Grenzkontrolle unterziehen musste, um den Ostteil der Stadt besuchen zu dürfen. Das war Blixa stets zu kompliziert gewesen, und außerdem hatte er „anderes zu tun". Er wollte

Blixa Bargeld named his band Einstürzende Neubauten after the collapse of the New Berlin Congress Hall (locally known as the *pregnant oyster*). They were the spearhead of a new generation of unconventional musicians who radically opposed the established music industry, they were described as the *Geniale Dilletanten* (ingenious dilettantes).

Although Blixa had no school qualifications, no job and no flat, he formed one band after the other, then he began to explore the industrial wastelands of West Berlin. He found a remote empty space inside of an Autobahn bridge, and used it as place to play music, even without owning much in the way of instruments or equipment. He used anything he could get his hands on. To him, the place had something magical about it, because it had an "unbelievable acoustic quality".

This cramped empty space was forty meters long, but only one and a half meters high, which meant that Blixa had to stoop over to maltreat his guitar, while heavy goods vehicles roared overhead. As he himself put it, "under such conditions, it was rather difficult to play music that had something to do with the peace movement".

For Blixa, West Berlin was "ground zero", a strange but creative island that was different from all other cities. The rents were far below the average of the Federal Republic of Germany and you could live on a bare minimum of money, which made the city attractive, not only to many men fleeing from West Germany Army, but also to those people from different countries, who were unable to discover themselves back home.

Since I was British, it was quite easy for me to cross over the border at Checkpoint Charlie or Friedrichstrasse in to East Berlin. I just had to pay five Deutsch Marks for a day visa and exchange the obligatory twenty five Deutsch Marks into East German monopoly money (with which I usually bought useless commie propaganda materials, like busts of Lenin and Marx). By contrast, if a West Berliner wanted to visit the eastern part of the city, they had to go to a specially designated place, fill out a form in advance and then wait three days before receiving their entry permit, they usually had to go through a daunting border control before being allowed in too. All this was much too complicated for Blixa,

▶ Blixa Bargeld

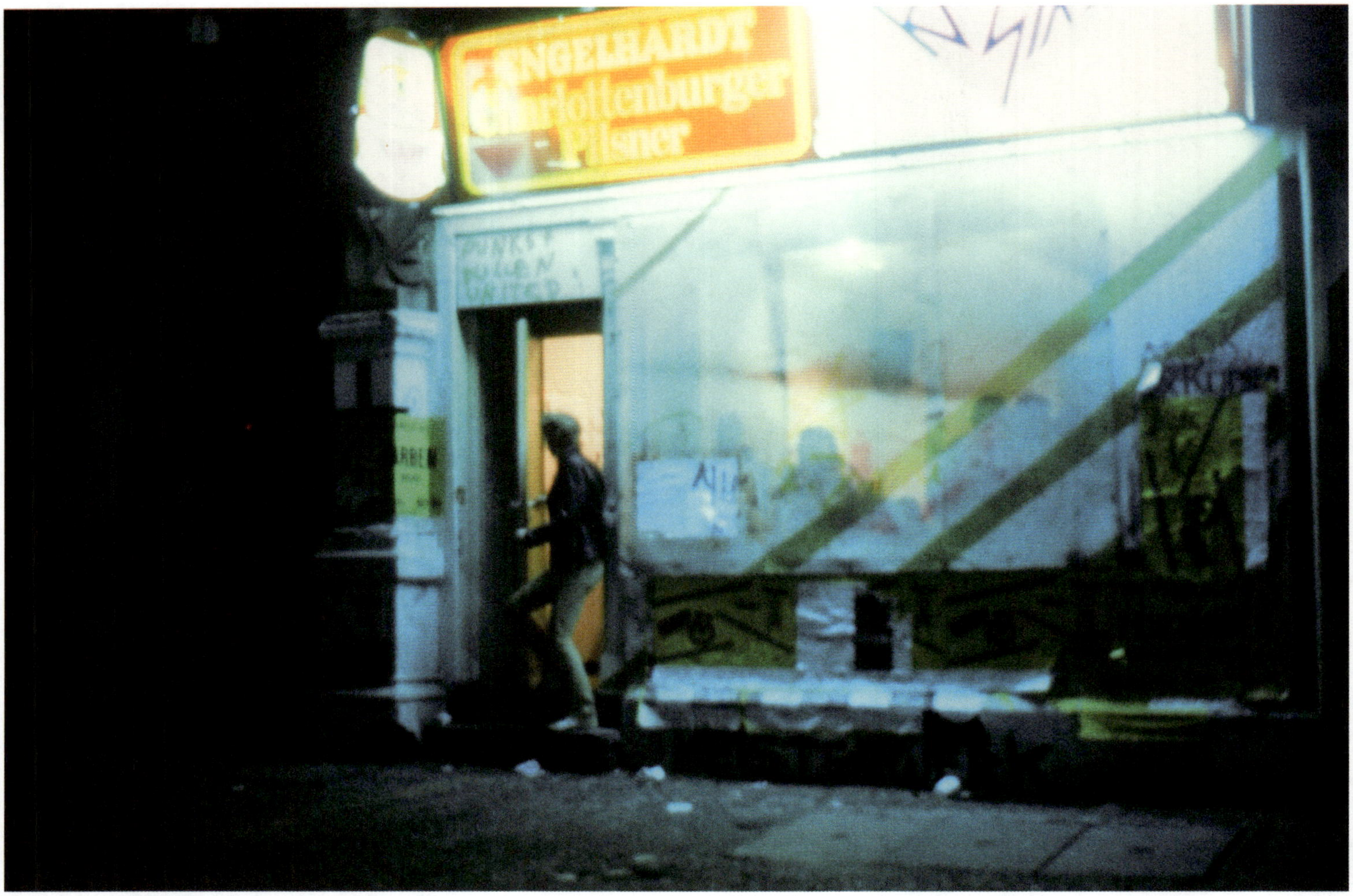
ENGELHARDT
Charlottenburger
Pilsner

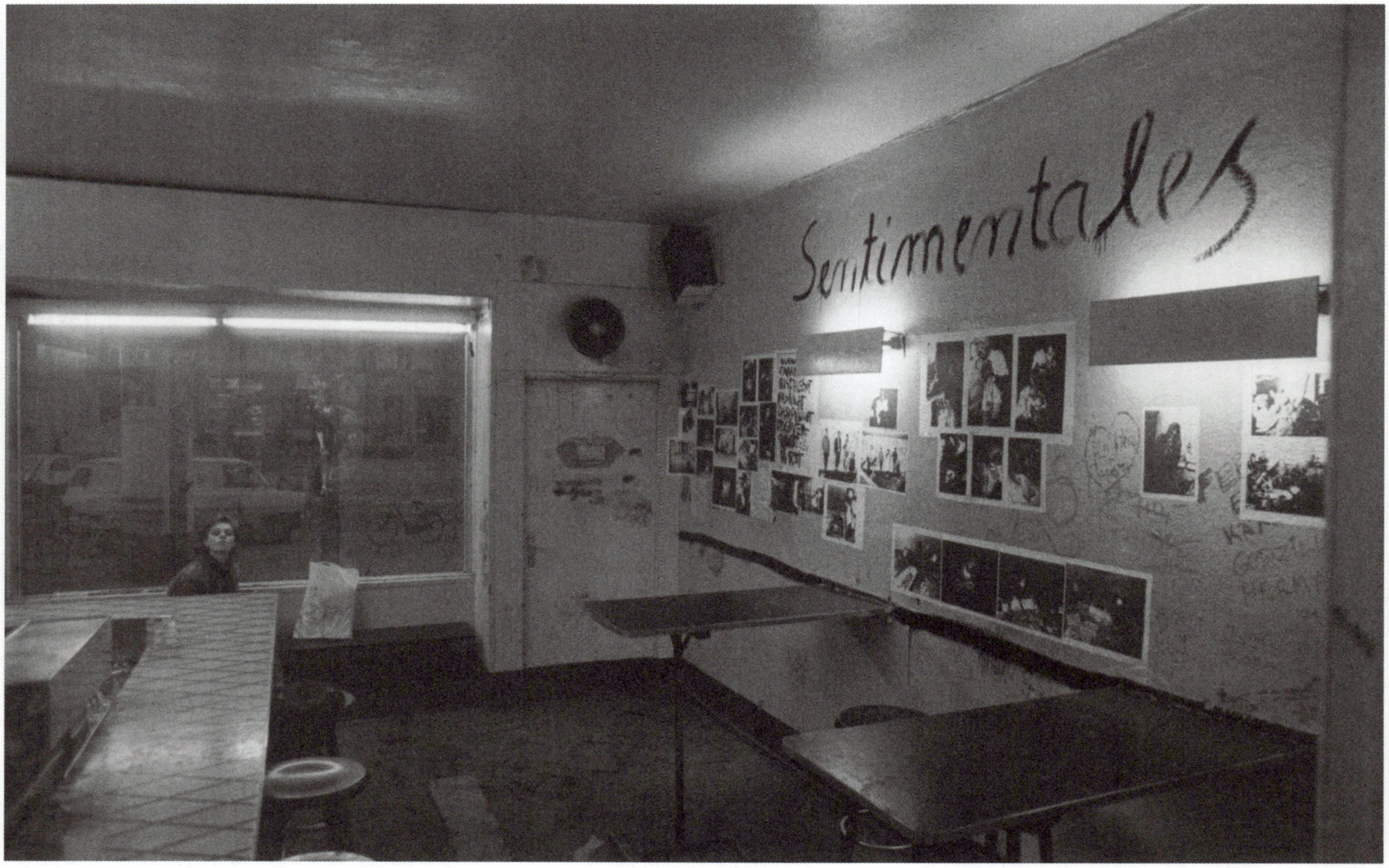
Sentimentales

einen Ausflug nach Ost-Berlin nicht drei Tage im voraus planen, und er sah auch keinen Grund, „eine Grenze zu passieren, um nach Berlin zu kommen" — wobei die DDR-Grenzer ihm mit seinen punkigen Gummistiefeln, den strubbeligen Haaren und diesem Heroin-Chic ohnehin die Einreise verwehrt hätten.

Er lebte halt gerne in dieser „novembergrauen, traurigen Stadt", deren andere Hälfte er nicht kannte. Nachdem er eine Zeit lang im Tali-Kino Karten abgerissen hatte, wenn dort die *Rocky Horror Picture Show* lief, oder im Café Anderes Ufer und im Mitropa als Barmann gejobbt hatte, stand er im Risiko, einem kleinen Club an den Yorckbrücken, hinterm Tresen und füllte die Leute mit Wodka ab. Im Risiko traf ich auch Leute wie Christiane F, das Mädchen vom Bahnhof Zoo, die schon kurz darauf zum Umfeld der Einstürzenden Neubauten zählte und auch in *Decoder* mitspielte, einem Film von Muscha und Klaus Maeck, der in Hamburg einen Punk-Plattenladen namens Rip Off betrieb.

Das Risiko war sehr typisch für das damalige Berlin. Es war der perfekte Absturzladen nach einem Konzertabend und sog jede Art von alternativen Künstlern an. Der bewusst erlebte Augenblick, die künstlerische Freiheit und Kreativität waren den meisten tausend Mal wichtiger als ein langfristiger oder kommerzieller Erfolg. Das ungeschriebene Motto lautete: Einfach machen.

Es ging nicht darum, *wie* man etwas machte, sondern *dass* man etwas auf die Beine stellte. Bands wie Leben & Arbeiten wurden nur für ein paar Auftritte gegründet und anschließend wieder aufgelöst. Jeder spielte mit jedem in ständig wechselnden Formationen — es war ein einziger musikalischer Inzest. Die Einstürzenden Neubauten schlugen auf Stahlträgern und Waschmaschinentrommeln herum. Wolfgang Müller von der Performance-Gruppe Die Tödliche Doris setzte einen pfeifenden Wasserkessel wie ein Instrument ein. Und bei Dimitri Hegemanns *Atonal*-Festival im SO 36 oder beim Festival der Genialen Dilletanten im Tempodrom trat auch ich mit meiner Gruppe Die Unbekannten auf.

Dass in Berlin wieder der Bär steppte wie zuletzt in den Zwanzigerjahren, vernahm man schon bald auch in

and besides, he said he had "other things to do". He said he just couldn't plan a trip to East Berlin three days in advance, and he didn't see a reason why anyone should have to "cross over a border to get to the other part of Berlin", and in his case - with his punk wellies, his extreme haircut and heroin-chic look - they probably wouldn't have let him in anyway. Blixa was quite content to live in what he described as this "November grey, sad city" whose other half he didn't know. After a brief spell as the doorman at the Tali Kino, he worked at the Anderes Ufer Café and at the Mitropa, and later he tended the bar at Risiko, a small club near the Yorckbruecken, where he made sure most of his clients ended under it. At Risiko, I also met many interesting people, like Christiane F. - the girl from Bahnhof Zoo - who was soon part of the Einstürzende Neubauten gang, she appeared with William Burroughs and Mufti in a early surveillance film called Decoder, by Muscha and Klaus Maeck who ran a punk record shop in Hamburg called Rip Off.

Risiko was quite a unique club, and the typical kind of haunt for Berlin's more nocturnal residents. It was the clubbers terminus, a perfect post-concert, after-hours bar where, if you managed to survive the night, you would inevitably end up at some stage. This little place attracted all kinds of alternative artists. Most of these people lived only for the moment absorbing the artistic freedom and creativity of the city, its clubs and bars. For most of them however, this flexibility and urge to be creative in some way, was much more important than long-term commercial success. There was no pressure to be popular. People were creative simply to express themselves. You didn't give it much consideration or worry about the consequences. Our unwritten motto was: just do it. It wasn't a question of how you did something but rather simply that you did something. Bands like Leben & Arbeiten were thrown together for a handful of gigs and then disbanded. It appeared like everyone was playing with everybody else, in ever changing combinations, it was more like musical incest, and it was wholly unconventional. Einstürzende Neubauten performed with steel girders, scrap metal, building site materials, old washing machine drums and general rubbish. Wolfgang Müller, from the art-performance group, Die Tödliche Doris *(Deadly Doris)*,

◄ Perfekter Absturzladen – das Risiko

84-85: Die Tödliche Doris
86-87: Christiane F und F.M. Einheit von den Einstürzenden Neubauten

England. Als meine Freundin Muriel Gray nach West-Berlin kam, um ein Special über die Berliner Szene für die ITV-Sendung *The Tube* zu drehen, kam sie aus dem Staunen nicht mehr heraus. Während man sich in Großbritannien darauf beschränkte, in einer einzigen Gruppe zu spielen, wechselte man in Berlin von einer Band zur anderen, als würden alle in einer einzigen riesigen Band Musik machen. „Von außen", so Blixa Bargeld, „wirkte es vielleicht so, als sei das alles geplant gewesen. In Wirklichkeit waren es nur zwei Dutzend Leute — in wechselnden Kombinationen." Gudrun Gut war dabei eine entscheidende Figur. „Wenn ihre Bandkolleginnen auch nur für zwei Wochen in Urlaub fuhren", erinnert sich Blixa in *B-Movie*, „hat sie die Zeit genutzt, um noch eine Band zu gründen." Als Musikerin Karriere zu machen, stand für sie gar nicht zur Debatte: „Hier war das Motto, alles neu erfinden und gucken, was geht."

Ich zeigte Muriel die Stadt und wir hauten richtig auf die Kacke. Der coolste Laden war zweifellos der Dschungel, in dem auch David Bowie und Iggy Pop ein paar Jahre zuvor verkehrt hatten und der Ur-Rasta Jimmy Bamba Platten auflegte. Dorthin zog es all die mega-hippen Leute, doch es zog sie auch alle wieder aus dem Dschungel raus und hinein ins Berliner Nachtleben. Denn die Szene schlief nie — jedenfalls nicht nachts. Niemand wollte etwas verpassen, man ging von Club zu Club, kam kurz nach Hause, wusch sich und zog wieder los.

In einer ehemaligen Dönerbude auf der Potsdamer Straße betrieben zwei Mädels, Cassia und Lucy, die ich aus dem Risiko kannte, einen „abstrakten" Frisörsalon — Penny Lane. Tagsüber wurden in dem winzigen Ladenlokal Kopf- und Schamhaare frisiert und nachts gab es Kunstausstellungen, experimentelle Konzerte und Performances. Es gab keine Toilette, nur ein Waschbecken, das sowohl zum Haarewaschen als auch zum Urinieren diente.

In die Bhagwan-Disco Far Out auf dem Kudamm wurde ich wegen meines harten, wenig hippieartigen Aussehens hingegen nie reingelassen. Dort tanzten Sanyassins und Hippies, die Disco war bekannt als idealer Abschleppladen und eine florierende Einnahmequelle des sexbesessenen Gurus aus Poona.

used a whistling kettle on stage as an instrument, and because our performances were rubbish, but considered to be avant-garde, I also played at Dimitri Hegemann's Berlin Atonal-Festival at the SO36, or at the Geniale Dilletanten Festival at the Tempodrom, with my band, Die Unbekannten. Berlin hadn't been this creative, or abstract, since the era of the Weimar Republic in the twenties and thirties and soon our alternative music scene became attractive news in the English media too. When my friend and TV presenter, Muriel Gray, came out to Berlin to film a special for the popular ITV programme The Tube, she just couldn't help but be amazed. In Britain, musicians limited themselves to playing in one single band, while in Berlin people regularly moved from one group to the other, it was almost like everyone was playing music together in one massive band. Blixa Bargeld explained it like this "Viewed from the outside, it seemed like everything had been planned this way. In reality, there were only about two dozen people – performing in variety of combinations." Gudrun Gut played a decisive role in all this. "When her band colleagues went on holiday for two weeks," recalled Blixa in *B-Movie*, "she used the time to put together a new band." Her career as a musician was certainly not up for debate, her motto was simply "re-invent everything and see what works."

I showed Muriel around the city. One of the coolest places at this time was arguably Dschungel, a club where David Bowie and Iggy Pop would occasionally hang out and the legendary African DJ, Jimmy Bamba played records. This stylish place attracted a very fashionable crowd, but its clientele were also part of Berlin's alternative nightlife. The scene never slept – at least not at night. You didn't want to miss a thing, you went from club to club, came home briefly, washed and then went out again.

In a former kebab shop on Potsdamer Straße, two girls I knew from Risiko, Cassia and Lucy, ran a rather abstract hair dressing salon called Penny Lane. During the day, you could have your hair trimmed - both the hair on your head and your pubic hair - and at night, they put on art exhibitions, experimental concerts and performances. There were no toilets, only a sink and that was used for both washing hair and also as a urinal.

89-94: Lucy Weisshaupt und Cassia Hecker im Penny Lane

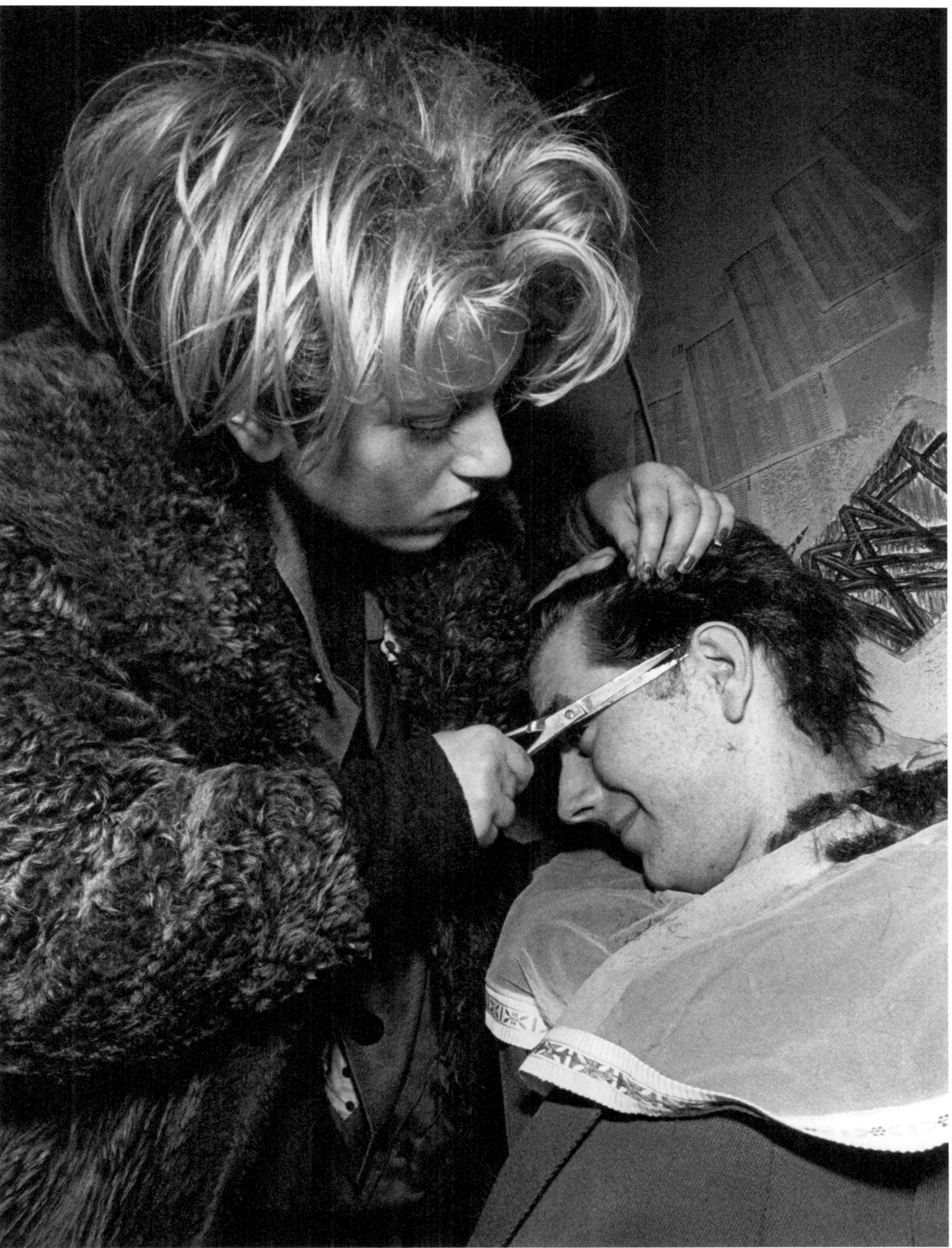

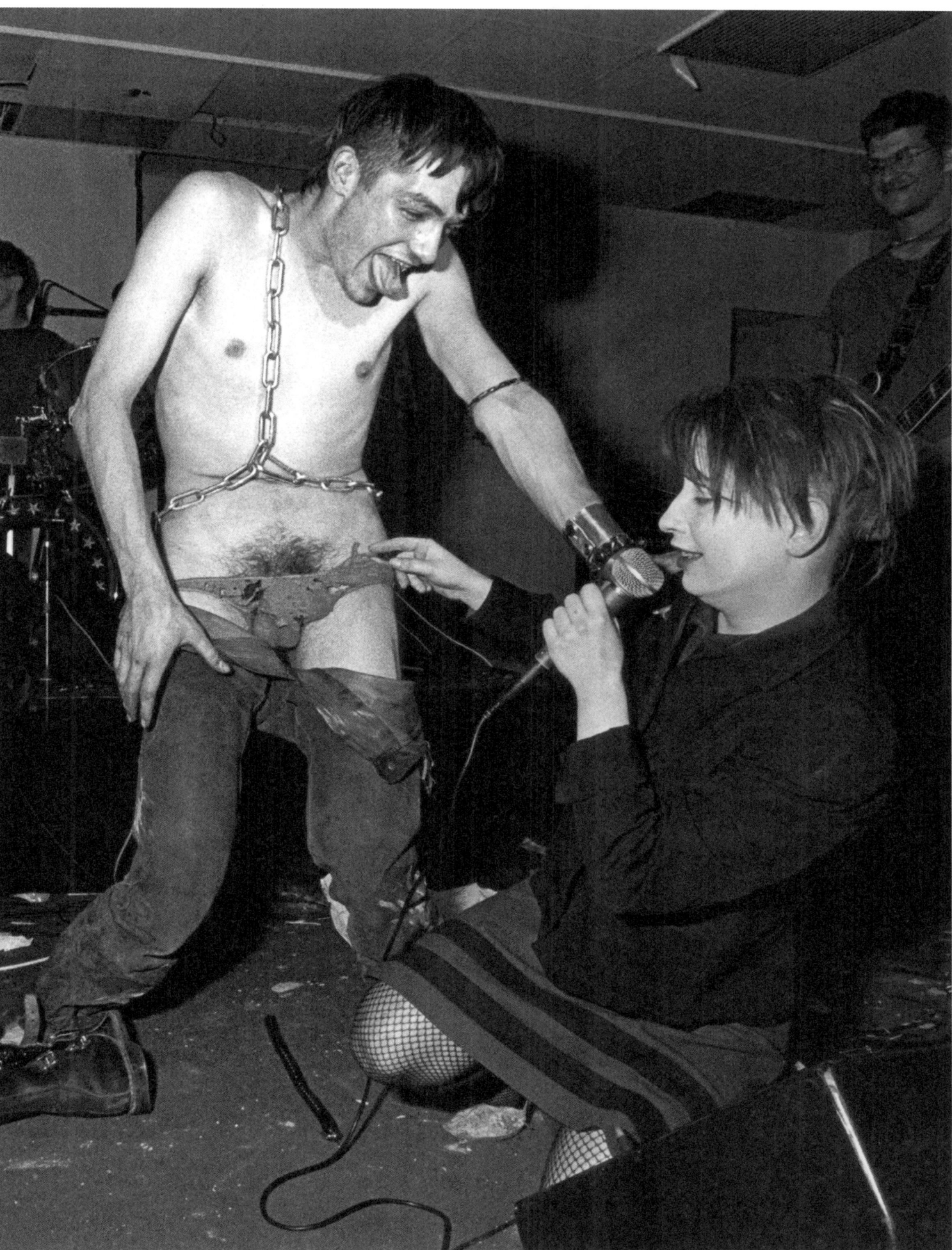

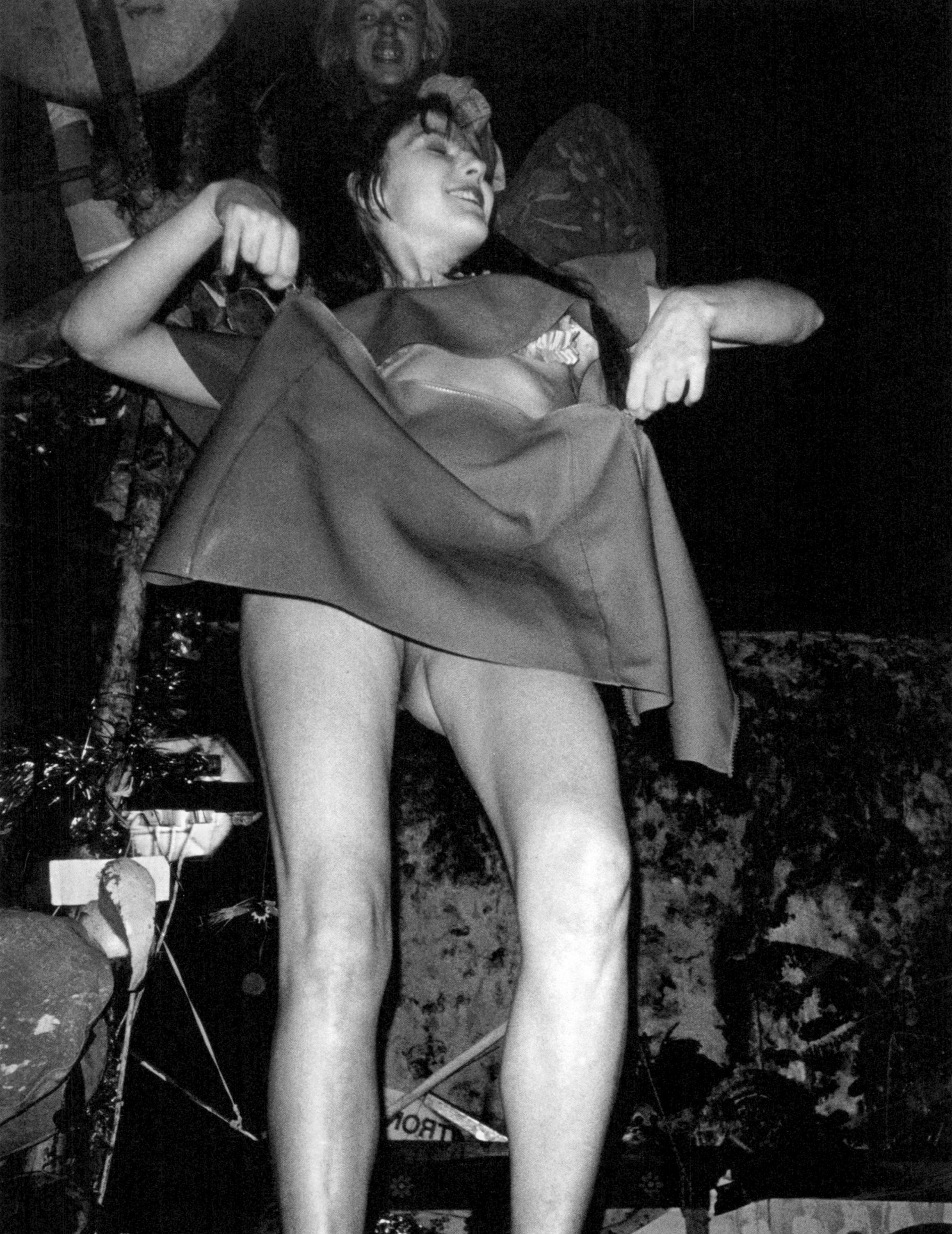

West-Berlin erfüllte dir einfach jeden Wunsch und das Leben war höchst exzessiv: Es gab ständig Partys, Drogen, Sex und Musik. Und am Ende stürzte man dann im Risiko ab, dem Treffpunkt der Untoten, der schon bald einen weiteren Stammgast bekam — Nick Cave.

Diesen australischen *Gentleman* hatte ich erst kürzlich kennengelernt, als Malaria! im Vorprogramm seiner Band Birthday Party aufgetreten war. Nach ihrem Gig in der Music Hall am Walther-Schreiber-Platz war Nick fasziniert von Berlin. Er wollte von mir alles über die Stadt wissen: Wie das Leben in Berlin ist, oder ob es schwer sei, eine Wohnung zu finden. Ich hatte in den höchsten Tönen von der Stadt geschwärmt und eher nebenbei angeboten, er könne bei mir kurz wohnen, bis er eine eigene Wohnung finde, wenn er mal nach Berlin käme. Er hing damals aber in England mächtig durch, und so klingelte es ein paar Wochen später plötzlich bei mir und Nick Cave stand unangemeldet mit zwei Koffern vor meiner Tür: „Da bin ich."

Was sollte ich tun? Ich ließ ihn bei mir wohnen, bis er etwas Besseres fand. Damals wusste ich noch nicht, dass er sich in Elisabeth Recker von Monogam Records verliebt hatte, einem Label, das Platten von Die Unbekannten und Die Haut und Singles von obskuren „Projekten" wie P1/E, Mono/45 UPM, Vorgruppe oder Frauen für schlechte Tage (Rainy Day Women) veröffentlichte. Sie war mit mir und meinem Freund Alistair Gray zum Konzert von Nicks Birthday Party gegangen, und der Legende nach soll Nick sie vorne am Bühnenrand stehen gesehen und sich auf der Stelle in sie verliebt haben. Pow! Pow! Pow! Eines Tages tauchte überraschend eine Frau bei mir auf, die sich als Nicks Freundin Anita vorstellte und fortan ebenfalls bei mir wohnte. Kurz darauf zog Nick bei dem Filmstudenten Christoph Dreher ein, der bei Die Haut Bass spielte und dessen Wohnung in der Dresdener Straße 200 qm groß war und ihm genug Platz bot, um sich zu entspannen. Anita Lane überließ er einfach mir.

Die Wand von Nicks neuem Zimmer war durch einen Vorhang in ein Arbeits- und ein Schlafzimmer unterteilt, das er mit seiner Sammlung gotischer deutscher Malereien dekorierte. Die Gaspistole, die er im Film *B-Movie* in

For some unfathomable reason, I was never allowed into the Bhagvan-Disco *Far Out* on Kurfuerstendamm, I suspect it was probably because of my dark, military and not very hippie-like appearance. Everyone there wore orange or red coloured clothing and so I guess refusal was guaranteed when I turned up there looking like the gestapo in a long leather coat, shirt, tie, boots and jodhpurs. Apparently, this was the place where alternative religious Sannyasins and hippies would dance to all kinds of trippy music, but in reality, this discotheque was known more for being the ideal pick-up joint, as well as a blossoming source of income for the sex-obsessed millionaire guru from Poona.

It appeared like West Berlin fulfilled almost every desire and life could be extremely excessive: there were constant parties with unlimited drugs, sex and music. And eventually after a long night out, you would always end up at Risiko, the meeting point for the undead, which would soon have another regular customer — Nick Cave.

I first met this Australian Gentleman when Malaria! supported his band The Birthday Party. After their gig at *The Music Hall* in Steglitz, Nick had become fascinated by Berlin. He wanted me to tell him everything about the city, what life in Berlin was like and whether or not it was hard to find a flat. I spoke highly about the city, praising its merits, like cheap booze, cigarettes, drugs and accomodation and I proposed he should come out and live with me for a while until he found his own place. I guessed he was at a bit of a loose end in England, and a few weeks later, my doorbell rang and Nick Cave was standing there, with two suitcases: "Here I am."

What could I do? Obviously, I let him stay with me in my shabby little flat until he could find something suitable. At that time, I didn't know it, but Nick had in reality fallen in love with Elisabeth Recker, my label manager from Monogram Records. Her label released the records of my band Die Unbekannten, as well as those from Die Haut and singles from more obscure projects like P1/E, Mono/45 UPM, Die Vorgruppe, or Frauen für schlechte Tage (Rainy Day Women). She had gone with me and my friend Alistair Gray to The Birthday Party gig and, according to legend, Nick saw her standing at the front of the stage and immediately fell in love with her. Love at first sight. Pow! Pow! Pow!

96-97: Die Tödliche Doris
98-99: Tequila-Wettsaufen im Risiko

Händen hält, gehörte allerdings nicht ihm, sondern Gudrun Gut, und wie im Film zu sehen ist, war er genauso erstaunt wie der Zuschauer, als er sie auf seinem Tisch entdeckte. Nick Cave lebte etwa drei Jahre in Berlin und wurde sofort von der einheimischen Kunst- und Kulturszene vereinnahmt. Die Szene war bunt gemischt und neben Musikern und Malern zählten auch Dichter und Filmemacher dazu. Nick erlebte in der Tat eine sehr aufregende Zeit. Denn Berlin war auch die Endstation von The Birthday Party; nachdem ihr Bassist Tracy Pew gestorben war, gründete Nick zusammen mit Mick Harvey, Thomas Wydler und Blixa Bargeld eine neue Band, The Cavemen, aus denen schließlich The Bad Seeds wurden. Blixa und Nick hatten sich schnell angefreundet und verbrachten viel Zeit miteinander. Gemeinsam führten sie einen „Krieg gegen den Schlaf", wie Blixa zu sagen pflegte. Ein bisschen unheimlich kam Nick mir aber schon vor: Als er bei mir wohnte, stand er nachts immer auf und grölte wie ein Zombie.

In meiner kleinen Bude begann Nick auch, eine Story über den australischen Outlaw Ned Kelly zu schreiben, die ein paar Jahre später mit Guy Pearce in der Hauptrolle verfilmt wurde. „Berlin hat mein Leben wirklich verändert", bekräftigt er heute. „Dort habe ich das nötige Selbstbewusstsein entwickelt, genau das zu tun, was ich will, und mich nicht um die Meinung anderer Leute zu kümmern."

Then one day, the doorbell rang and there stood a red headed girl who claimed she was Nick's girlfriend Anita. This suddenly looked like things were going to get really complicated. She also ended up briefly living with me. Shortly after her arrival, Nick moved into the flat of Christoph Dreher, a handsome film student who played bass with Die Haut, he had a massive 200 square meter industrial appartment on Dresdener Strasse, which offered plenty of room to relax. Nick left Anita with me to deal with and so one night at Risiko, I managed to convince the music journalist Oliver Schunt (the Vampire from to Lysanne Thibodeau's film, *bad blood for the vampyr*) to take her under his wing. Nick's new appartment was separated by a curtain which divided his "room" into an office and a bedroom which he decorated with gothic German paintings ripped from a book. The gas-pistol that he held in his hands in the film *B-Movie* actually didn't belong to him, but to Gudrun Gut, and as one can see in the film, he was as surprised as the audience usually is, when he came across it lying on his desk. Nick Cave lived for about three years in Berlin and was immediately embraced by the local art and cultural scene. This scene was very diverse and in addition to musicians and painters, there were also poets and filmmakers. It was a turbulent time for Nick. For Berlin was also to become the terminus for his band, The Birthday Party; after the death of their bassist Tracy Pew, Nick decided to put together a new band with Mick Harvey, Thomas Wydler and Blixa Bargeld - The Cavemen – a band which eventually became know as The Bad Seeds.

Blixa and Nick became friends straight away and spent a lot of time with each another. Together, they waged a "war against sleep", as Blixa succinctly put it.

In my flat, Nick also began to write a story, he said it was about the Australian outlaw Ned Kelly, which would be made into a film years later, with Guy Pearce in the starring role. "Berlin really changed my life," he affirms today. "There, I was able to develop the necessary self-confidence to do what I want, and not to worry about the opinions of other people."

◀ Wolfgang Müller und Blixa Bargeld

102-103: Blixa Bargeld und Nick Cave im Fahrstuhl des Hansa-Studios
104-105: Blixa Bargelds Zimmer

▲ Blixa und Beate Bartel
 (Malaria!)
▼ Checkpoint Charlie
▶ Blixa Bargeld

108-109: Nick Cave live im SO 36

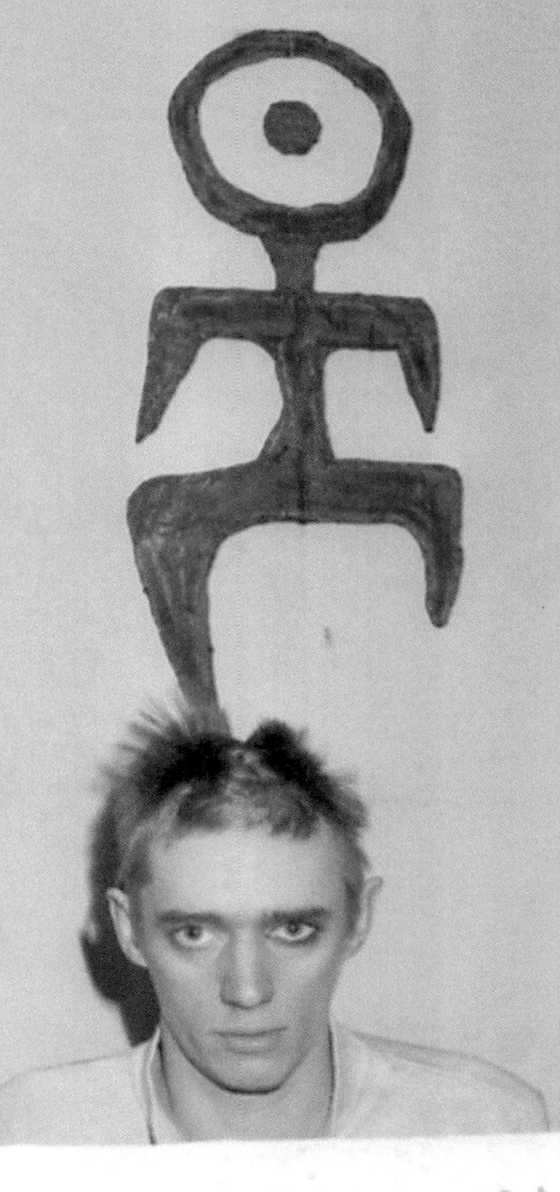

DU BIST AUF SENDUNG
YOU'RE ON THE TELLY

Nach dem Tod von Ian Curtis wollte ich auf keinen Fall wieder zurück nach Manchester, doch ich fragte mich, ob meine Zukunft wirklich in Berlin lag. Meine Frage wurde jedoch schnell beantwortet, denn niemand beschrieb die Schönheit dieser Stadt besser als die neugewellte Gruppe Ideal in ihrer Hymne „Ich steh auf Berlin".

Ideal hatten einen sehr eigenen Sound, der überhaupt nicht amerikanisch oder englisch klang, und spielten zu Beginn ihrer Karriere auf einem Solidaritätskonzert für die immer größer werdende Szene der Hausbesetzer. Als der Berliner Senat ihr ein Ende bereiten wollte und einige Häuser gleichzeitig räumen ließ, kam es natürlich zu wütenden Protesten. Und als die Teilnehmer einer spontanen Demonstration vor der Polizei auf die Potsdamer Straße flüchteten, die nicht für den Verkehr gesperrt war, passierte etwas Schreckliches: Der 18-jährige Klaus-Jürgen Rattay rutschte beim Versuch, auf einen Bus aufzuspringen, aus und wurde von ihm mitgeschleift und tödlich verletzt. Ich war zufällig in diese Auseinandersetzung zwischen den Hausbesetzern und der Polizei hineingeraten, weil ich an der Kurfürstenstraße aus der U-Bahn gestiegen war, um nach Hause zu kommen, und ich war total schockiert. Während man in England Squatter nicht von der Polizei vor die Tür setzen lassen konnte (ein entsprechendes Gesetz wurde erst 2011 verabschiedet), hatte der Berliner Senat keine bessere Idee, als die Polizei aufzurüsten. Die Bullen bekamen nun Ausrüstungen aus Kevlar-Hartplastik und sahen darin aus wie Robocops. Und auch unter den Hausbesetzern und ihren Sympathisanten gab es eine immer größere Bereitschaft zur Militanz. Der Tod von Klaus-Jürgen Rattay schockierte alle. Als Polizei und Staatsanwaltschaft auch noch ein Ermittlungsverfahren gegen den toten Rattay wegen Landfriedensbruch einleiteten, radikalisierte sich die Szene, die in Berlin viel organisierter war als daheim in England. Für die Medien war das natürlich ein gefundenes Fressen.

Ideal traten mit ihrer Musik etwas los, was als Neue Deutsche Welle in die Geschichte einging und den Punk-Underground überrollte. Schon bald gab es kaum noch eine deutsche Gruppe, die nicht deutsch sang.

Annette Humpe von Ideal hatte zunächst englische Texte

After Ian Curtis died, I knew I didn't want to return to Manchester, but I asked myself if my future was really going to be in Berlin. My question was soon answered however, since no one described the beauty of Berlin better than the new group Ideal, in their cynical homage to the city, "Ich steh auf Berlin" (I adore Berlin).

Ideal had a truly unique new wave style, they sounded really German and nothing like an American or a British band. At the start of their career, they regularly played solidarity concerts for the increasingly growing squatter scene. When the Berlin Senate decided to forcibly evict the squatters and clear out the houses for demolition, there were enraged protests. One afternoon, as the participants of a spontaneous demo fought with the police on Potsdamer Strasse, which hadn't been closed off, something really tragic happened. During the protest, 18 year old Klaus-Jürgen Rattay, slipped as he tried to climb onto a bus, it ran over him and dragged him along the road and he was fatally injured.

By chance, I witnessed this particular conflict between the squatters and the police because I had just come out of the Underground at Kurfürstenstrasse and was on my way home. I didn't see the accident itself, but I was totally shocked when I heard about it a few hours later. In England, the police back then were not allowed to simply evict squatters (a change in that law was passed only in 2011), but for whatever reason, the Berlin Senate didn't have any better idea than to rearm the police force. The police now wore Kevlar armour and looked like Robocop. In return, the squatters and their sympathisers, became more militant. Klaus-Juergen Rattay's death shocked everyone. When the police and the public prosecutor's office launched a judicial inquiry against the deceased Rattay for breach of the peace, the squatters simply became organised and much more radicalised. Naturally, the media lapped it up.

Ideal had certainly kicked off something with their particular style of music. It would eventually be recognised as the beginnings of Neue Deutsche Welle (German New Wave) a popular sound which was rolling over the punk underground. Soon, there was hardly a German new wave group left that didn't sing in German.

Annette Humpe, the lead vocalist of Ideal, had originally

▶ Annette Humpe, Uli Deuker und F.J. Krüger von Ideal
114-115: Die Neonbabies Inga und Annette Humpe im Exxcess
116-117: Die Humpe-Sisters

CESSEX
Kingbees
So.
The Kin
arleenes
Mo.
The
y Ritmo
gbees
eenes
itmo

So.	The Kingbees		So.	The Kingbees
Mo.	The Darleenes		Mo.	The Darleenes
Di.	Timmy Ritmo		Di.	Timmy Ritmo
Mi.	One Way Subway			One Way Subway

ESS EXCESS EXCESS
STRASSE 101 KURFÜRSTENSTRASSE 101 KURFÜRSTENSTRASSE 101

Präsentiert:

gesungen, weil das viel einfacher war und sie sich hinter einem Wort wie „Baby" gut verstecken konnte. Ihre deutschen Texte waren jedoch viel direkter und sie kam sich zunächst nackt vor, weil ihr Publikum jedes Wort verstand und sofort merkte, ob jemand log oder glaubwürdig war.

So wie Die Ärzte, eine neue Fun-Punkband, die gerade durchstartete und die ich Muriel Gray wärmstens ans Herz legte, als wir einen Bericht mit Musik aus beiden Teilen Berlins für die britische Kultursendung *The Tube* produzierten. Die Band war erst ein paar Monate alt und noch ganz frisch. Es war ihr erster internationaler Fernsehauftritt, und wir nahmen einen Song von ihnen auf, den sie extra für unsere Sendung über Nacht geschrieben hatten: „Eva Braun", ein sehr sarkastisches Liebeslied, mit dem auch Engländer etwas würden anfangen können.

Ihr Gitarrist Farin Urlaub führte Muriel in das prunkvolle Café Möhring am Kudamm aus, das in den Zwanzigerjahren der Mittelpunkt der dekadenten Berliner Koks-Szene gewesen war, wie man sie aus dem Filmmusical *Cabaret* kennt. Damals waren im Möhring Zwerge mit Koks auf einem am Kopf befestigten Tablett herumgelaufen, doch nun saßen dort nur Omas, die Kaffee tranken und Kuchen aßen. Zum Beweis, dass die betagten Damen an den Nachbartischen die Überlebenden jener Koks-Ära waren, wies Farin Muriel mit schalkhaften Augen auf ihre Nasen hin. Und auch sonst war er nicht auf den Kopf gefallen. Als Muriel ihn nach den Aussichten für Berliner Bands befragte, von denen ja kaum eine außerhalb Deutschlands berühmt war, und ob sich das nun groß ändere, gab er sich ebenso skeptisch wie charmant: „Schwer zu sagen. Die Einstürzenden Neubauten sind in Großbritannien bekannt geworden, weil sie neue Musik machen. Einen ähnlichen Erfolg werden wir dort nie haben, weil ihr die Musik, die wir machen, schon habt: von den Undertones oder den Buzzcocks, und die sind besser als wir." Es sei auch schwierig für eine deutsche Band, international berühmt zu werden, denn um ehrliche Musik zu machen, müsse man deutsche Texte schreiben. „Und die versteht keiner." Farin Urlaub irrte. Man konnte mit deutschen Texten sehr wohl international erfolgreich sein, denn es gab Jim Rakete, einen Fotografen, Talent Scout, Produzenten und Manager, der Nina Hagen zum Erfolg verholfen hatte

sung English lyrics, because she said it was easier and she could hide behind words like "baby". Her German lyrics however, were by contrast, much more direct and she felt naked because the audience could understand every word and could immediately tell if someone was lying, or was believable.

Same with Die Ärzte (*The Doctors*), a new fun-punk band which had recently formed from the remnants of the punk band Soylent Gruen, that I warmly recommended to Muriel Gray for our special Berlin edition of legendary British cultural programme *The Tube*. The band was only a few months old and virtually unheard of. This was to be their first ever television appearance and I convinced them that this was their chance to make a lasting impression and to write a song that the British audience would never forget. We included a song of theirs that they had written especially for our programme the night before, *Eva Braun* - a really sarcastic love song that they thought british TV viewers would be able to relate to.

Their guitarist Farin Urlaub brought Muriel to the prestigious Café Möhring on the Kurfürstendamm, which in the 1920's, had been the centerpoint of the decadent Berlin cocaine scene, something like depicted in the film musical *Cabaret*. Back then, dwarfes with trays of cocaine fixed on their heads, would go around feeding the indulgent clientele, but now only grannies seemed to be sitting about drinking coffee and eating cake. Farin made a remark with mischievous grin that Muriel should look at *their* noses. Otherwise, he was pretty honest. When Muriel asked him about the outlook for most bands in Berlin, he explained that most were barely known outside of Germany, and whether that would now significantly change, he was as skeptical as he was charming: "That's difficult to say…". He said, "The Einstürzende Neubauten are now known in Great Britain because they're playing new music. We can never have that kind of success there, because the style of music that we make, you already have: bands like The Undertones or The Buzzcocks, and they're better than we are." He thought it would be difficult for a German band to become internationally famous, since the music had to be authentic and for that, the lyrics also had to be sung in German. "… and no one will understand us."

▶ Die Ärzte Bela B und Farin Urlaub
120-121: Die Ärzte
122-123: Ärzte-Fan Mark Reeder

und in dessen Kreuzberger Fabrik, einem Kreativlabor, dessen Name ein wenig an Andy Warhols Factory erinnern sollte, die Produktion auf Hochtouren lief. Wie fast jeder West-Berliner war auch Rakete ein Kind von AFN und Coca-Cola und kulturell von den USA beeinflusst worden. Er hätte aber auch Waschmaschinen oder Kühlschränke verkaufen können, denn Berlin war für ihn eine „klassische amerikanische Kolonie, was das Rockprodukt anbelangt". Musik war für ihn nur ein Produkt, und mit der unprofessionellen Avantgarde-Szene konnte er sich nicht anfreunden. Berlin war in seinen Augen „einfach eine sehr kaputte Stadt", weshalb auch die Musik, die dort gemacht würde, „sehr kaputt" sei.
Nena kann er damit nicht gemeint haben, denn mit ihnen gelang ihm der größte Treffer. Sie schafften das, woran viele nicht mal im Traum glaubten: Mit deutschen Texten zu Weltstars zu werden. Die letzte Berlinerin, der das gelungen war, war Marlene Dietrich gewesen. Und das war schon verdammt lange her.
Zu dem Song von den „99 Luftballons" war ihr Gitarrist Carlo Karges durch ein Konzert der Rolling Stones in der Waldbühne inspiriert worden, als die Stones Luftballons aufsteigen ließen. Es war ein großartiger, naiver Pop-Song, den alle gut fanden, denn Nena grenzten sich nicht von der Berliner Post-Punk-Szene ab und es gab auch keine Animositäten zwischen der Pop- und der Avantgarde-Szene: Auf einer Dampferfahrt tanzte ihre Sängerin Gabriele „Nena" Kerner ausgelassen mit Gudrun Gut. Das German Fräuleinwunder war eine Lizenz zum Gelddrucken und durfte auch in meiner Plattensammlung nicht fehlen.
Für ihren Berlin-Report wollte Muriel unbedingt auch eine DDR-Punkband haben, die radikal und systemkritisch war. So eine zu finden, war aber gar nicht so leicht, wie sie es sich vorstellte. Denn offiziell gab es keinen Punk in der DDR, weil der mit Arbeitslosigkeit assoziiert wurde, und die gab es ja bekanntlich nicht im Arbeiter- und Bauernstaat. Als ich mit der Straßenbahn durch Ost-Berlin fuhr, erspähte ich zufällig ein paar Jugendliche mit Gitarrenkoffern, die wie nette Punks von nebenan aussahen. Ich lief ihnen hinterher und sprach sie an. Anfangs war ich ihnen suspekt und sie schauten mich

Yet Farin Urlaub was mistaken. You could indeed be internationally successful with German lyrics. Jim Rakete, a photographer, talent scout, producer and manager, who had helped Nina Hagen achieve international success and in whose Kreuzberger "Fabrik" - a creative laboratory which modelled itself on Andy Warhol's Factory – was in full production mode. Like almost every West Berliner, Rakete grew up on a diet of AFN and Coca-Cola, and was culturally influenced by the USA. I guess he could have probably sold washing machines or refrigerators, for Berlin was to him simply a "classic American colony, with regard to Rock products". Music appeared to be just another commodity for making money for him; he certainly couldn't relate to what he considered the unprofessional avant-garde scene. Berlin for him was "a fucked up city", and accordingly, most of the music that was made here, well that was "fucked up", too. He obviously didn't mean Nena of course, because she was his most successful artist. With her he had phenomenal success. She was able to achieve what most could never even dream of, she became a global star, singing in German! The last woman from Berlin who managed to do that was Marlene Dietrich. And that was a hell of a long time ago. Her song „99 Luftballons", was inspired by a concert of the Rolling Stones at the Waldbühne amphitheatre, where they released hundreds of helium balloons into the air. Her guitarist Carlo Karges was there and he wrote the song shortly after.
It was a wonderfully catchy, naïve pop song that everyone seemed to love, and because Nena didn't disconnect herself from the Berlin post-punk scene, there was no animosity between her brand of pop and the avant-garde scene. On a boat trip *(for Joerg Hoppe's birthday)* Gabriele „Nena" Kerner danced enthusiastically together with Gudrun Gut. She was so successful, it was as if this German fraeuleinwunder had a license to print money – and indeed, she was an indispensable part of my own record collection.
Initially, for The Tube, I was hired to select the bands, research locations and organise the shoot, but the moment Muriel saw me in my dark leather Gestapo coat, shirt, tie and trilby, she was awestruck. She was insistant and exclaimed there was going to be no way around it "You're on the Telly!"

▶ Nena und Gudrun Gut
126-127: Carlo Karges und Susanne Gabriele Kerner von Nena

skeptisch an, weil ich in meinem Zwanzigerjahremantel und mit meinem Trilby-Hut wie ein Mafioso aussah. Sie spielten in einer Band, Jessica, und probten in einer Schule. Sie wollten so klingen wie The Police. Bei der FDJ kannte jedoch niemand eine Gruppe namens Jessica, weil die keine Einstufung hatte, eine staatliche Genehmigung, live aufzutreten oder Platten aufzunehmen. Man bot mir stattdessen Silly, City, Karat, Stern Meissen und die Puhdys an. Doch die wollte ich nicht, weil sie viel zu alt waren und nicht repräsentativ genug für eine britische Jugendsendung. So begann ein Katz-und-Maus-Spiel, das sich sehr in die Länge zog. Offiziell durfte ich Jessica gar nicht kennen, sodass unsere Korrespondenz streng geheim bleiben musste. Ich riet ihnen, sich bei der FDJ zu melden und ihr mitzuteilen, sie hätten gehört, dass das britische Fernsehen sie filmen wolle. Sie sollten die FDJ-Leitung bitten, ein gutes Wort für sie einzulegen. Meine Geduld zahlte sich schließlich aus und ich konnte Jessica in *The Tube* vorstellen. Ich war so aufgeregt, dass ich kaum ein Wort über die Lippen kriegte.

Für ihren ersten Fernsehauftritt bekam jedes Bandmitglied die stolze sozialistische Gage von 16 Ost-Mark, obwohl wir ein paar Tausend D-Mark dafür an eine DDR-Behörde überweisen mussten. Also schmuggelte ich 500 D-Mark in einer Musikcassette über die Grenze, damit sie eine ordentliche Gage erhielten. Ihr Auftritt war schließlich ein historischer Moment: Es war das erste Mal, dass eine DDR-Band, und dann auch noch eine ohne Einstufung, im britischen Fernsehen gezeigt wurde. Jessica machte daraufhin im Osten rasch Karriere, verschwand aber wieder von der Bildfläche, ohne dass es jemandem auffiel, als die Mauer fiel.

Eigentlich hatte ich ja nur für die Sendung recherchieren, Bands auswählen und Drehgenehmigungen besorgen sollen. Ich half auch gerne, aber als Muriel mich in meinem Gestapo-Ledermantel sah, hieß es plötzlich: „Du bist auf Sendung."

Dass ich einmal eine eigene Sendung im englischen Fernsehen haben würde, hätte ich, als ich noch in Manchester lebte, nicht zu träumen gewagt. Doch meinen Berlin-Enthusiasmus nahm mir ein erzkonservativer

For this *Tube Berlin Special,* Muriel really wanted an East German punk band, something that was radical or perhaps critical of the stark stalinist system. She couldn't imagine how difficult it was to even find such a band. Officially, punk didn't exist in the GDR, because it was associated with the failings of capitalism and the resulting unemployment and of course, such things didn't exist in the fully employed *workers' and farmer's State.*

I was getting desperate, but one day I had a lucky break. Whilst sitting on the tram in East Berlin, I spotted a couple of young lads with guitar cases, who looked from their appearance like new-wavey types. I jumped off the tram and ran after them. They were curious, but obviously really suspicious of me because I looked a bit like a Mafioso in my black frock coat from the twenties and my trilby hat. They said they played in a new wave band called Jessica, and that they practiced in a school. They told me they wanted to sound like The Police. I immediately, thought this just might be the kind of thing I was looking for and something I could probably get past the authorities. Nice eastie kids playing bland but aceptable music. Unfortunately, no one at the FDJ (Free German Youth) had ever heard of Jessica, because they weren't officially recognised and didn't have the proper classification, i.e. an official authorisation to play live performances or to make records.

Instead, the East German officialdom offered me bands from their regular stable of aging artists, such as Muck, Silly, City, Karat, Stern Meissen and the Puhdys. I told them I didn't want these kind of artists, because they were much too old and not really representative enough of the GDR for a British youth programme. I wanted someone young! So began a cat-and-mouse game that continued for quite a few months. Officially, I wasn't allowed to even know that Jessica exsisted, so my correspondence with the band had to remain strictly secret. I advised them to approach the FDJ and let them know that they had heard a rumour that British television wanted to film them. They should ask the FDJ supervisors to put in a good word for them. My patience finally paid off and in the end, I was able to present Jessica on *The Tube*. It was a mgnificent coup. I was so excited that we had pulled it off, that I could hardly speak, let alone translate for Muriel.

◀ Nina Hagen im Britischen Sektor
130-131: live im Quartier Latin
132-133: an der Berliner Mauer

Nachbar meiner Eltern sehr krumm, der im Zweiten Weltkrieg bei Mountbattens Royal Marine Commandos gedient hatte, die für ihre ebenso mutigen wie waghalsigen Einsätze gegen Deutschland gerühmt wurden. Er hatte auch 1977 die Polizei gerufen, als Königin Elizabeth II. ihr silbernes Thronjubiläum gefeiert und ich ein God-Save-The-Queen-Poster der Sex Pistols in das Fenster meines Zimmers gehängt hatte. Als ich meine Eltern nun zu Hause in Manchester besuchte, gab er mir unmissverständlich zu verstehen, was er davon hielt: „Du bist in Deutschland? Du lebst unter den Feinden!"

Als meine Eltern dann 1984 erstmals nach Berlin kamen, zeigte ich ihnen auch den Ostteil der Stadt, der sie an die Nachkriegszeit daheim erinnerte. Es gab keinen Verkehrslärm, weil es kaum Autos gab. Die Leute waren nett aber unauffällig gekleidet, und der Ersatzkaffee und das Aluminiumbesteck waren in fast jedem Café „wie früher". Meine Mutter meinte, ich hätte die beste Entscheidung getroffen, die ich habe treffen können, und fügte hinzu: „Wenn ich so jung wäre, würde ich auch hierher ziehen."

An den Wochenenden hing ich fast immer im Metropol ab, wenn dort Gay-Disco war, um die neuesten HiNRG-Scheiben und US-Importe zu hören, die der DJ Chris von einem Plattenladen im Kudamm Karree bezog. Das Metropol war damals, was heute das Berghein ist — ein Ort, an dem alles möglich zu sein schien. Um über die Runden zu kommen, jobbte ich dort auch im Loft als Türsteher für Monika Döring. Oder ich spielte den Reiseführer für Bands und ging mit ihnen Kaffeetrinken und zeigte ihnen die Sehenswürdigkeiten in beiden Teilen der Stadt.

Von meinen Leuten hatte niemand die Absicht, eine Mauer zu vernichten. Denn die Mauer war längst nicht nur eine Art Lebensversicherung für West-Berlin, sondern auch eine ideale Projektionsfläche für Inszenierungen, die sich künstlerisch mit der geteilten Stadt auseinandersetzten. Als der anti-imperialistische Schutzwall 1986 seinen 25. Geburtstag feierte, schmissen die Notorischen Reflexe, eine Multimedia-Gruppe von Ghazi Twist, Christoph Doering und Knut Hoffmeister, die aus den Nachrichten ihre eigene Wahrheit montierte, eine wilde Party, auf der sie Musik, Filme, Malerei und Geschriebenes zu einer Show

For their first ever television appearance, I discovered each band member would receive the generous socialist participation fee of 16 East German Marks *(about 1,50 Euro)*, even though we had paid a couple of thousand Deutsch Marks to the GDR authorities to film this event. So I smuggled 500 Deutsch Marks into East Berlin, hidden inside a music cassette, so they could at least receive a decent wage.

Their performance was indeed an historical moment: it was the first time that an East German band – and one that had no classification either – had appeared on British television. Afterwards, Jessica became very popular in the East, but virtually disappeared without trace once the Wall fell.

It would have never crossed my mind to have my own TV programmes on British telly if I had lived in Manchester. In fact, my enthusiasm for Berlin deeply offended our conservative next door neighbour who had served during World War II in Mountbatten's Royal Marine Commandos - who were well known for their equally courageous, as well as daring missions against Nazi Germany. He was a true royalist and had actually called the police when I had hung a Sex Pistol's 'God Save The Queen' poster in my bedroom window on the day of Queen Elizabeth's Silver Jubilee in 1977. So when I now went back to visit my parents in Manchester, he made it unequivocally clear as to what he thought about my disgusting defection, "You're in Germany? … You're living with the enemy!"

When my parents finally came to visit me in West Berlin for the first time in 1984, I also showed them the Eastern part of the city too, which they loved. It reminded them of the post-war period back home. There was almost no traffic noise, since there were hardly any cars. The people were dressed nicely but modestly and the *Ersatzkaffee* and aluminium cutlery in almost every Eastie café reminded them "how things used to be in the 50's". My mother surprised me by saying that moving to Berlin was the best decision that I could have made and added, "If I were as young as you, I would also move here."

On the weekends, I usually went to Metropol, the largest gay disco in Europe. Here I could dance and listen to the latest electronic, Hi-NRG and US import records that the

vermischten und so ihre Ideen ausdrückten. Die Mauer war für sie der Rahmen einer grenzenlosen Freiheit — was dahinter lag, war den meisten völlig egal.

Der Berliner Senat hatte natürlich einen ganz anderen Freiheitsbegriff als wir, musste uns letztlich aber gewähren lassen, weil wir sonst fortgegangen wären und die Stadt ausgeblutet zurückgelassen hätten. West-Berlin brauchte uns, um seine Existenz zu legitimieren, und wurde so zum einzigen Ort, an dem man frei denken und sich keine Grenzen setzen musste, sondern sich einfach ausprobieren konnte. Es ging nicht darum, Erfolg zu haben, sondern allein darum, etwas zu machen — ob das jemandem gefiel oder nicht, war egal. Man hatte eine Idee für eine Performance, ein Festival oder einen Auftritt, und dann hat man einfach losgelegt. Das finanzielle Risiko war gering; mein Proberaum kostete damals zum Beispiel gerade mal 20 Mark Miete im Monat.

Wir glitten wie auf Schienen durch die Nacht, aßen „Reeder's Digestives", von mir gebackene Haschkekse, und schnieften billiges Speed oder warfen Microdots ein, stark dosierte Mini-LSD-Trips. Heroin gab es nahezu überall, doch das war nichts für mich, Koks hingegen nur selten, und es war auch viel zu teuer. Kurz nach meiner Ankunft in Berlin hatte ich in einem Club, in dem Hippies und No Waver verkehrten, mal ein sehr schräges Erlebnis gehabt: Das sehr gemischte Publikum hatte völlig zugedröhnt auf dem Boden gesessen und die komplette Seite einer Platte von Tangerine Dream gehört. Das war 1978 im Sound gewesen, einer Disco in der Nähe des Nollendorfplatzes, die man mir empfohlen hatte, weil sie cool sei. Es war auch der Lieblingsladen von Christiane F. gewesen, und es gab dort alle Arten von Drogen. Sogar vor dem Eingang hatten mich zwiespaltige Typen gefragt, ob ich Trips, Speed oder Haschisch kaufen wollte. Im Sound hatten die Kids psychedelische Musik gehört, und in ihren eng gestreiften Hosen und Jeans-Jacken hatten sie wie Hippie-Punks ausgesehen.

DJ, Chris brought from his own record shop in the Ku'damm Karree. Metropol was back then, what Berghein is today: a place where literally *everything* and *anything* seemed possible. To make ends meet, I did all kinds of odd jobs. On the west side, no one had the intention of pulling down the Wall… at least none of the people I knew. For the Wall had become the guarantor of eveything we held sacred about Berlin. Not only was it the life insurance for West Berlin but it was also the ideal projection screen for all kinds of artistic activity which confronted the issue of living within the divided city. Such as the twenty-fifth anniversary celebration to commemorate the building of the so-called anti-fascist protection wall, by the Notorische Reflexe, a multimedia group formed by artists Ghazi Twist, Christoph Doering and film maker Knut Hoffmeister. To celebrate the *Mauerstadt,* they threw a wild party in which they set fire to the wall. They were known for assembling their own version of the news, which was a mixture of edited official broadcasts, in which they would integrate music, film, animation, painting and spoken word to fully express their ideas. For them, the wall was the framework for unlimited freedom without borders and what lay beyond the wall was utterly irrelevant.

The Berlin Senate had a completely different definition of freedom than we did, but unofficially they permitted us to do whatever we wanted, since otherwise many of us would probably have the left the city to bleed. West Berlin needed all us weirdos and draft dodgers to justify its existence and it became the only place where a person could think freely, with no limitations, but where things could simply be tried out. It wasn't about being successful, but merely about the act of doing something and it certainly didn't matter if anyone liked it or not. If you had an idea for a performance, a festival or a gig – then you would just do it. The financial risk was always minimal, Berlin was cheap. For example, my rehearsal room, cost me only 20 Deutsch Marks rent per month.

We glid through the nights as if on rails, especially after eating some of my own home-baked "Reeder's Digestive" hash biscuits, or we sniffed cheap speed, or dropped the occasional LSD trip.

136-137: Inga Humpe von den Neonbabies

Heroin was readily available, but it didn't interest me and cocaine was very scarce and much too expensive. Drugs have always played a huge role in Berlin. Shortly after my arrival in Berlin, I had a really strange experience in a club where hippie-punks and No-Wave types usually hung out. This diverse and pretty fucked up crowd were all sitting cross-legged on the metal dance floor listening to the entire side of a Tangerine Dream record. That was back in 1978 in Sound, a notorious discotheque near Nollendorfplatz that had been recommended to me because it was apparently cool. In reality, it was drug central and Christiane F.'s favorite haunt, probably because you could get every kind of stimulant imaginable in there. In fact, directly in front of the entrance, stood a line of very dodgy looking blokes, who would whisper to the passing clubbers if they wanted to buy trips, smack, speed or hash. They listened to quite a lot of psychedelic music in Sound, and I thought many were obviously struggling with their identities, wanting to be fashionably punk, but scared to throw off their old hippie styles, so you would see them wearing tight stripey trousers with jeans jackets and half shorn off hair. I thought most looked just like hippie-punks.

◀ Inga Humpe
▲ Tempo

140: Matador
141: Frieder Butzmann
142-143: Ideal und Spliff

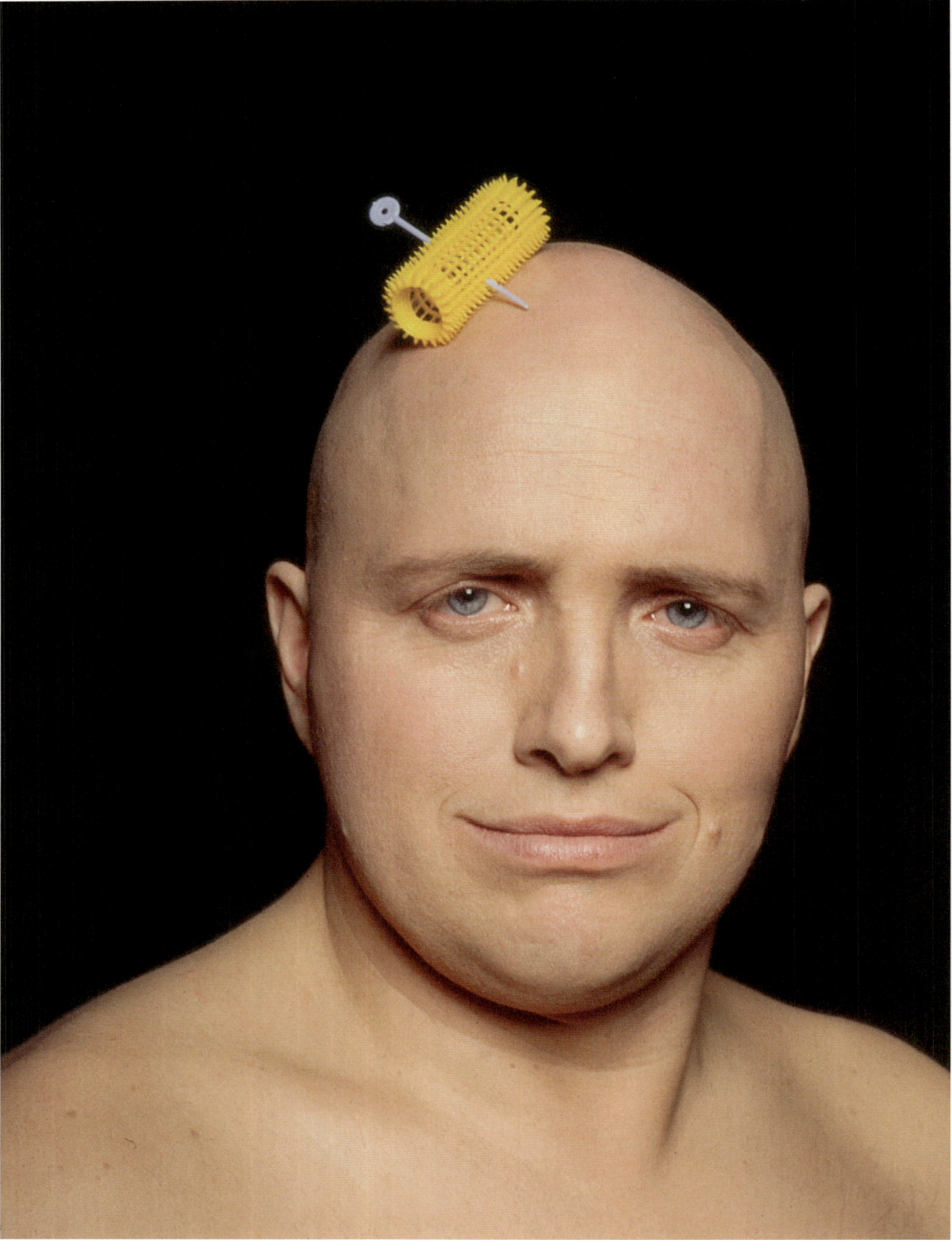

EIN SCHICKSAL NAMENS MONIKA
A FATE CALLED MONIKA

Alistair Gray und ich trugen uns schon seit längerem mit dem Gedanken, das Image unserer Band Die Unbekannten zu verändern. Wir wollten weg von dem depressiven und dunklen New-Wave-Sound und ihn in einen lustigen Hi-Energy-Disco-Sound umwandeln. Da kam Bernard Sumners Angebot, 1984 mit New Order auf Tour zu gehen, gerade recht. Wir formierten uns neu, Die Unbekannten bekamen zwei neue Mitglieder, und Shark Vegas war geboren.

Die Unbekannten waren die allererste Band gewesen, die im Loft gespielt hatte, und Shark Vegas traten dort oft im Vorprogramm von Freunden aus England auf. Das war wohl unser Schicksal.

Das Schicksal hieß Monika Döring und sie betrieb diesen legendären Club im Metropol am Nollendorfplatz. Ich hatte sie ein paar Jahre zuvor kennengelernt, als sie das Festival *Rock Against Junk* mit Gang of Four und Blurt veranstaltete. Zu meinem großen Erstaunen hatte sie im Backstagebereich des von ihr organisierten Anti-Drogen-Festivals gesessen und einen Joint gedreht. Monika war verantwortlich für die besten Konzerte, die in den Achtzigerjahren in West-Berlin stattfanden, fühlte sich aber auch der Berliner Szene gegenüber verpflichtet: „Natürlich ziehen New Yorker und englische Gruppen erst mal die Leute ins Haus. Und dann kriegen sie bei mir immer gleich noch eine Berliner Gruppe mitgeliefert — ob sie wollen oder nicht."

Als wir mit New Order auf Europatournee waren, wollte Bernard Sumner unsere erste Single „You Hurt Me" in Conny Planks Studio in der Nähe von Köln produzieren. Es war für uns alle ein sehr aufregendes Erlebnis, bei dem berühmten Produzenten von Kraftwerk, DAF und Ultravox aufzunehmen. Leider ließ er sich aber kaum blicken und spielte lieber Tischtennis, während sein Tontechniker Dave Hutchins mit einem furchtbaren Hexenschuss auf einer Holzliege vor dem Mischpult lag. Er schrie immer vor Schmerzen, wenn er uns mitteilte, was wir als Nächstes tun sollten. Das Endergebnis klang entsprechend grauenhaft. Vor einem Konzert in München trafen wir bei unserer Ankunft im Hotel den Nena-Keyboarder Uwe Fahrenkrog-Petersen im Fahrstuhl. Er erkannte Bernard und lud uns zu

Alistair Gray and I had long been toying with the idea of changing the sound and image of our band, Die Unbekannten. We wanted to get away from our depressing, dark sound and move into the exciting and entertaining Hi-Energy electronic disco sound. So, when in 1984, Bernard Sumner offered us the chance to go on tour with New Order, the timing just seemed perfect. We reformed the band, acquired two new members and Shark Vegas was born.

Die Unbekannten were the very first band that had ever played in the Loft, supporting Die Toten Hosen, and now Shark Vegas would also become the opening act for many bands from England. That was our destiny.

And destiny came in person of Monika, Monika Döring, who ran the Loft, the legendary live venue in the Metropol theatre on Nollendorfplatz. I worked there as doorman. Naturally, I also became the tourguide for her visiting bands, taking them for coffee, or showing them the sights on both sides of the walled city.

I had met Monika a few years before, when she was the promoter of the *Rock Against Junk* festival, with Gang of Four and Blurt. I was astonished and highly amused, when I saw her sitting backstage at her own anti-drugs festival rolling a joint! Monika was responsible for some of the best concerts that took place in West Berlin during the eighties, but she also felt a sense of responsibility for the entire Berlin music scene, "People are first drawn to see the bands from New York and England, but then they also get a group from Berlin as part of the package, whether they like it or not."

During our European tour with New Order, Bernard Sumner decided he wanted to produce our first single "You Hurt Me" in Conny Plank's studio near Cologne. We were all full of excited anticpation, as we knew it was going to be a really thrilling experience for us all, recording with the renowned producer of Kraftwerk, DAF and Ultravox. Unfortunately, Conny had more important things to do, and preferred to play table tennis while his sound technician. Dave Hutchins, who was suffering from a painful slipped disc, would scream orders to us while lying on a wooden camp bed directly in front of the mixing desk. As you can

▶ Bernard Sumner (New Order)
148-149: New Order live im SO 36

einer Pool-Party von Nena und Udo Lindenberg ein. Um den Pool herum standen lauter Bonzen ihrer Plattenfirmen in feinen Anzügen, nippten am Wein und knabberten an Lachs- und Käsehäppchen. Rob Gretton wettete mit unserem Lichttechniker um 100 Englische Pfund, dass er es nicht wagen würde, einen dieser Schlipstypen in den Swimmingpool zu stoßen. Kurzentschlossen lief der zu einem von ihnen rüber und warf den armen Mann hinein, wobei der sich am Buffet festzuhalten versuchte, das somit ebenfalls im Pool landete. Oops! Wir verschwanden recht zügig. Am nächsten Morgen meinte der Kellner beim Frühstück zu uns: „Ihr hättet gestern Abend hier sein sollen. Da hat jemand den Hotelmanager in den Swimmingpool geworfen."

Die letzte Station unserer Europatournee war Berlin. Ein Heimspiel. New Order waren begeistert, wieder Berliner Boden unter den Füßen zu haben, und um mich zu provozieren, wollten sie ständig wissen, was mich an Berlin besonders reize. Ich ließ den Blick nachdenklich durch den Backstage-Raum schweifen und zeigte schließlich auf Ratten-Jenny, eine der ersten Berliner Punkettes, die in einem besetzten Haus am Winterfeldplatz wohnte und so genannt wurde, weil sie stets eine weiße Ratte auf ihrer Schulter trug. Sie war mit Nina Hagen und Wayne County befreundet, dem Sänger der Electric Chairs, der sich später einer Geschlechtsumwandlung unterzog und sich seitdem Jayne County nennt.

Wayne bzw. Jayne und Ratten-Jenny kannten sich aus dem Café Central am Nollendorfplatz, vis-à-vis vom Loft, und Jenny lief der Ruf voraus, sowohl den Maler Salomé von der Gruppe Geile Tiere als auch den zwischenzeitlichen Betreiber des SO 36, Martin Kippenberger, verprügelt zu haben. Wolfgang Müller verglich sie in seiner Chronik des Berliner Underground, *Subkultur Westberlin 1979 – 1989,* später mit anderen Szene-Größen wie Käthe B. oder Straps-Harry und bezeichnete sie als „Künstlerin ohne Werk". Und genau das war sie auch: Sie gehörte einfach dazu und beeindruckte New Order, als sie nach dem Gig aus ihrem BH ein paar während des Konzerts geborene Mäuse-Babys hervorzauberte. Dem hatten sie nichts entgegenzusetzen.

imagine, the finished result sounded fucking horrible. We had many adventures on this tour. After arriving at the Intercontinental hotel before our concert in Munich, we met Nena's keyboardist Uwe Fahrenkrog-Petersen in the lift. He instantly recognised Bernard and kindly invited us to a pool party which was being given by Nena and Udo Lindenberg. Standing around the pool were a flock of record label executives from her record company, all wearing fine suits, sipping wine and nibbling on canapes of salmon and cheese. Rob Gretton loathed this kind of corporate event and bet our lighting technician a hundred pounds that he wouldn't dare to push one of these well-dressed *bastards* into the swimming pool. Rob randomly pointed one out and suddenly, the techie ran over to his selected victim and pushed the poor fellow in the pool, who, in desparation, tried to hold onto the buffet table, but ended up pulling it in as well. Oops! We made a hasty exit. The next morning at breakfast, the waiter said to us, „You should have been here last night. Someone threw the hotel manager into the swimming pool."

The last stop of our European tour was Berlin. New Order were thrilled to be back in Berlin again and were looking forward to eating Schweinshaxe. During an interview (and in a feeble attempt to provoke me) they repeatedly questioned my motives as to what kept me in Berlin and insisted upon asking me what fascinated me the most about Berlin in the hope I would say something embarrassing. In this backstage area stood Rat Jenny, she was one of the first Berlin punkettes who lived in a squatted house near Winterfeldplatz. She got her nickname from a rat that she carried about on her shoulder all the time. She was friends with Nina Hagen and Wayne County, the lead singer of the Electric Chairs, who later had a sex change and became Jayne County.

Jayne knew Rat Jenny from Café Central on Nollendorfplatz, which was vis-à-vis from Loft, and Jenny had the notorious reputation of having beaten up both the artist Salomé from the group Geile Tiere, as well as the originator of the SO36, Martin Kippenberger. Wolfgang Müller, in his chronicle of the Berlin Underground, *Subkultur Westberlin 1979 – 1989,* compared her with other important figures

▶ Jayne County

Für den Kabelsender Musikbox, einen Vorreiter von MTV in Europa, sollte ich zum Start des Deutschen Kabelfernsehens eine Sendung organisieren. Mit Shark Vegas spielte ich auf dem Breitscheidplatz, und es war eine Ehre für uns, als erste Band überhaupt im Kabelfernsehen aufzutreten. Im Gegenzug wollte man mit uns ein cooles Video auf der Glienicker Brücke drehen, auf der hin und wieder hochrangige Ost- und West-Agenten ausgetauscht wurden. Ohne zu ahnen, wie aufwändig das werden und wie viel Zeit und Nerven mich das kosten würde, schaffte ich es dank meiner Kontakte zum American Forces Network (AFN) blitzschnell, eine Drehgenehmigung zu erhalten, und so drehten wir kurz vor Sonnenuntergang ein Video direkt auf der Brücke. Zu dumm nur, dass die Amis den Russen nichts davon gesagt hatten und die DDR-Grenzer nicht darüber informiert waren. Auf dem östlichen Teil der Brücke war schon bald der Teufel los, und statt unsere Karriere voranzutreiben, hätten wir fast den Dritten Weltkrieg ausgelöst. Der kommerzielle Durchbruch blieb uns jedoch verwehrt und Shark Vegas verschwanden trotz der Unterstützung durch New Order wieder in der Versenkung.

like the artist Käthe B. or Straps-Harry a weirdo tranny, calling her "an artist without portfolio". And that was exactly what she was: she was simply a part of the scene, and she certainly impressed New Order with her latest performance, when she pulled out a pair of freshly born baby mice from beneath her bra, that she said had been born during their concert. The band were speechless.

I was asked to organise another broadcast for a popular cable TV show called Musikbox, the forerunner of MTV in Europe. This programme was the run-up for the launch of cable TV in Germany. My band, Shark Vegas was invited to perform at Breitscheidplatz, and it was a huge honour for us to be the first thing ever to appear on German cable television. To promote the event, they also wanted us to film a cool video on the infamous Glienicker Bridge, near Postsdam. This was the historical East-West bridge, divided in the middle, where high profile spies like Gary Powers had been exchanged. Without understanding how difficult that would normally be to arrange, or how much paperwork would be involved, they urged me to try. Thanks to a friendly contact I had made at the American Forces Network (AFN), we were instantly granted permission and were able to film our video directly on the bridge. Dressed as tortured, exchanged spies, we performed our song "Love Habit" as the sun was setting. Unknown to us, the Americans hadn't informed the Russians that we would be making this video and so the GDR border police hadn't been told either. On the Eastern side of the bridge, they were all flapping. So instead of this being an important step in our careers, it suddenly looked like we were about to set off World War Three! Despite our recordings and the tour with New Order, commercial success unfortunately remained elusive to us and Shark Vegas eventually slipped away into obscurity.

▶ Cafe Central
154-155: Ratten-Jenny

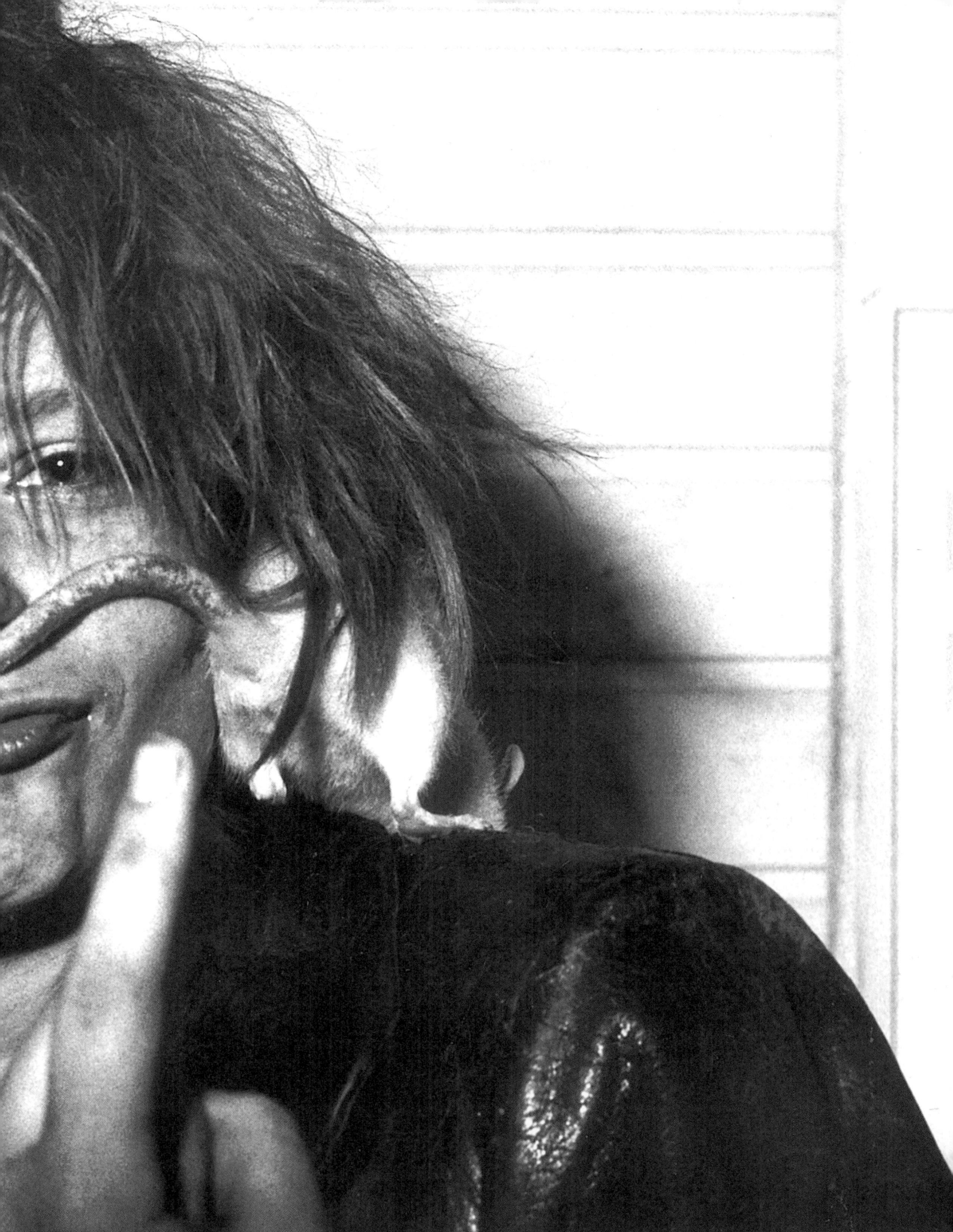

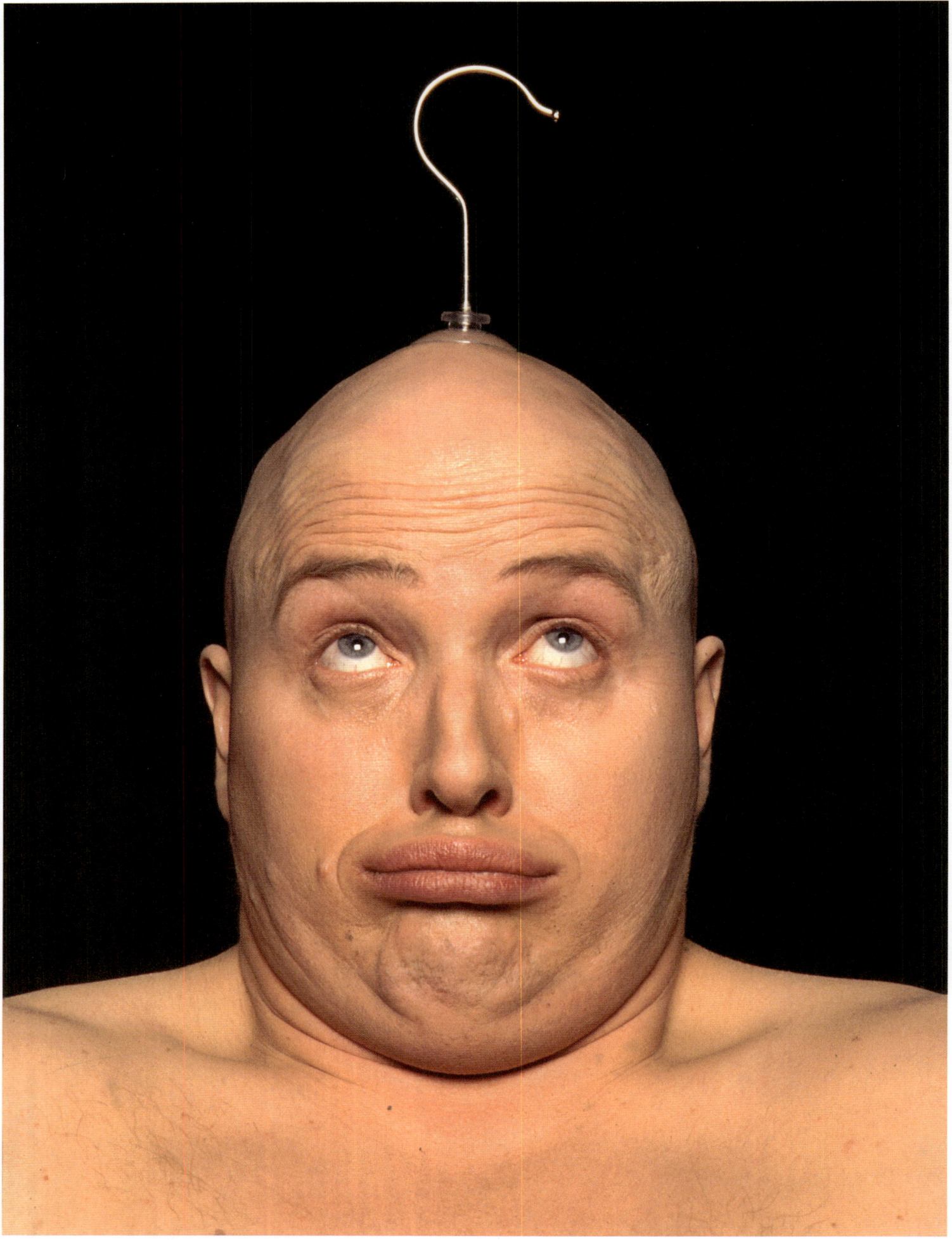

VII

DEMILITARISIERUNG DER MODE
DEMILITARISATION OF FASHION

Schon als Jugendlicher hatte ich mich immer in einem Army-Laden eingekleidet, weil meine Familie aus der Arbeiterklasse stammte und nie viel Geld für teure Klamotten hatte. So lief ich schon sehr früh in billigen, robusten Uniformhosen oder -jacken rum, die viele Taschen hatten, was sich später als ideale Kleidung erwies, wenn ich mit Malaria!, den Toten Hosen oder Shark Vegas auf Tournee war. In meinen Augen war das eine Demilitarisierung der Mode, ein Anti-Statement, und in Berlin konnte ich mein Faible für Uniformen voll ausleben. Mal lief ich in einem Hemd rum, wie es Berliner Polizisten 50 Jahre zuvor getragen hatten, und mal in einer NVA-Uniform, die ich aus der DDR hinausgeschmuggelt hatte. Die Deutschen fanden meinen Look zugleich super und komisch. Wenn ich in meinem langen schwarzen Ledermantel, zu dem ich ein aus den Vierzigerjahren stammendes Hemd und eine Krawatte trug, durch Berlin lief, zog ich viele Blicke auf mich und bekam nicht selten zu hören: „Ey, du siehst aus wie einer von der Gestapo!" Ich fand das aber total geil, damit die Leute zu provozieren, und trieb meinen Uniformfimmel immer mehr auf die Spitze.

Die meisten Berliner ignorierten meinen Spleen, von Touristen oder Fernsehteams wurde ich aber des Öfteren darauf angesprochen. Ihre blöden Fragen, warum ich Armeeklamotten trug, gingen mir schon bald auf den Geist. Wenn ich ihnen vorflunkerte, ich sei ein Militarist, guckten sie mich immer ganz ungläubig und irritiert an. Der Filmemacher Jörg Buttgereit fand mein Outfit hingegen äußerst interessant und engagierte mich als Schauspieler; vermutlich, weil ich meine Kostüme immer selbst mitbrachte. Dadurch war ich zwar auf gewisse Rollen festgelegt, aber seine Splatter Movies *Der Todesking* oder *Nekromantik 2*, in denen ich die männliche Hauptrolle spielte, landeten ohnehin regelmäßig auf dem Index, sodass meine Karriere als Schauspieler eigentlich schon vorbei war, bevor sie überhaupt angefangen hatte.

Tilda Swinton hatte da schon mehr Erfolg. Ich kannte Tilda als „army brat", wie sich die Tochter eines hochrangigen britischen Besatzungsoffiziers selbst beschrieb. Nachdem sie 1986 für Derek Jarmans Film *Caravaggio* erstmals

Even as a kid, I liked to wear army surplus clothes. I came from a working class background and although I dressed smartly, my parents never really had that much money to buy me fashionable or expensive clothing. So from a very early age, I knocked about in cheap, but sturdy army trousers or jackets, preferably ones with lots of pockets. This particular style of clothing proved to be ideal when I was on tour with Malaria!, the Toten Hosen, Die Unbekannten, or Shark Vegas. I never regarded military clothing as something demonic. To me it was merely practical. This was more of an anti-statement, the demilitarisation of fashion, and in Berlin, I discovered I could live out my fascination for uniforms to the limit. I would scour the second hand shops and I found plenty of stuff unavailable in Britain, like an old black shirt that was worn by the Berlin Police 50 years previously, and lots of Weimar republic clothing. I even got a one-stipe-no-stripe camouflage uniform of the NVA (National People's Army of East Germany)that I had taken great personal risk to smuggle out of the GDR. If they had caught me with that, I'd have probably been shot! Being British basically gave me a free pass to be bonkers and dress the way no German would ever dare. The Germans thought that I looked super, scary and funny at the same time. When I strolled though Berlin with my short hair, my long, dark leather coat, wearing a shirt from the forties and a tie, I knew it would provoke a reaction. Many people would simply stare at me and most would suffer in silence and say nothing, but occasionally, mainly at gigs, someone would come up and say, "Eh… do you know, you look like the Gestapo?" I found it hilarious to provoke the Germans in this way.

Most Berliners would just ignore my eccentricity, but more often than not, I would get quizzed by tourists or television crews. Their boring questions, always querying as to why I was wearing such brutal looking army clothes, eventually got on my nerves. Just to observe their reaction, I would tell them that I was a militarist! They would look at me increduluosly, with shock and disbelief. The notorius splatter film maker Jörg Buttgereit also knew I had all this crap and hired me as an actor; probably because I would bring my own costume. Accordingly, my roles were

vor der Kamera gestanden hatte, lebte sie eine Zeit lang in West-Berlin und drehte dort mit der Filmemacherin Cynthia Beatt den Kurzfilm *Cycling the Frame*, in dem sie mit dem Fahrrad an der Mauer entlangfährt. (Cynthia kannte ich ebenfalls: In ihrem Film *The Party* spielte ich einen besoffenen Gast.) Nachdem Tilda Swinton mit Filmgrößen wie Leonardo DiCaprio, Tom Cruise, Keanu Reeves und George Clooney zusammengearbeitet und 2007 einen Oscar als beste Nebendarstellerin erhalten hatte, wiederholte sie 2009 ihre Fahrradtour entlang der Berliner Mauer für Cynthia Beatts TV-Film *The invisible Frame* und wurde im selben Jahr Jury-Präsidentin der Berliner Filmfestspiele. Und als David Bowie 2013 einen Video-Clip zu seiner Single „The Stars (Are Out Tonight)" drehte, spielte sie darin seine biedere Ehefrau.

always somewhat limited, but he still used me. I appeared in two of his most controversial films *Der Todesking* and *Nekromantik 2*, where I played the male leading role. Both films were banned, so my career as an actor was essentially over before it had even begun.

Tilda Swinton would have more success as an actress. I knew Tilda as a self proclaimed "army brat". She was the daughter of a high-ranking British officer of the occupying forces. After she appeared in front of the camera for the first time in Derek Jarman's 1986 film *Caravaggio*, she lived for a while in West Berlin, where she shot a short movie, *Cycling the Frame*, for another film making friend of mine Cynthia Beatt, in which she rode her bicycle along the entire length of the Wall. I also appeared in one of Cynthia's films featuring Tilda, *The Party*, where I played a very drunken guest together with esteemed musician Simon Fisher-Turner. In comparison to mine, Tilda's career really took off, and she would later go on to work with many global filmstars such as Leonardo DiCaprio, Tom Cruise, Keanu Reeves or George Clooney, and in 2007 she won the Oscar for best supporting actress. A few years later, she repeated her bicycle tour around the now non-existant Berlin Wall in Cynthia Beatt's 2009 film *The invisible Frame*. In the same year, she was invited to be Jury President of the Berlinale - The Berlin International Film Festival -, and in 2013, when David Bowie made a video clip for his single "The Stars (Are Out Tonight)", she played his conservative wife.

160: ▲ Mark Reeder mit Elisabeth Recker und Alistair Gray
▼ ◄ im Shirt der Freien Deutschen Jugend
▼ ► bei der Sowjetischen Armee in Karlshorst
162-165: in russischer Pilotenuniform
166-167: Inga Humpe

DISNEYLAND FÜR DEPRESSIVE
DISNEYLAND FOR DEPRESSIVES

Blixa Bargeld war, als ich ihn kennenlernte, noch nie in Ost-Berlin gewesen. Was hinter der Mauer lag, interessierte ihn und die meisten genialen Dilettanten, Punks und Freaks nicht, die nach West-Berlin gekommen waren, um sich auf dieser Insel inmitten des roten Meers entfalten und ausleben zu können. Die DDR und der real existierende Sozialismus war ihnen viel zu spießig und erinnerte sie zu sehr an ihre Heimat, der sie mit Mühe und Not entflohen waren. Sie wollten einfach nicht vom Regen in die Traufe kommen, sondern fühlten sich wohl in dem Biotop im Schatten der Mauer.

Ich hingegen war sehr oft in Ost-Berlin, gemeinsam mit Joy Division und New Order, mit John Peel und vielen anderen Künstlern, aber auch mit meinen Eltern oder allein, und traf mich dort mit Freunden und Punks, die es im Arbeiter- und Bauernstaat offiziell gar nicht gab, und versorgte sie heimlich mit Musik aus dem Westen. Das Schmuggeln von Musikcassetten, die ich für sie aufgenommen hatte, war an sich nicht wirklich gefährlich, aber eine Strafe wäre sehr teuer gewesen. Und wenn man mich erwischt hätte, wäre ich wohl mit einem Einreiseverbot belegt worden. Ost-Berlin war auf eine faszinierende Art schäbig. Im Winter roch es penetrant nach Braunkohle und über allem waberte der Geruch von Zweitaktmotoren. Es kam mir vor wie eine Parallelwelt aus *Star Trek* und war eine Art Disneyland für Depressive. Ich liebte es.

Bei einem meiner ersten Besuche hatte ich in der U-Bahn einen jüngeren Typ gesehen, der etwas strubbelige Haare hatte, sonst aber ziemlich korrekt aussah. Ich erkundigte mich bei ihm nach Punk-Konzerten, aber er zuckte nur mit den Schultern und meinte, in Ost-Berlin laufe nichts: „So was gibt es nicht hier, das ist verboten." Ich konnte das kaum glauben, gab ihm meine Adresse und bat ihn, mir eine Postkarte zu schicken, wenn er etwas hören würde. Ein paar Monate später erhielt ich dann einen Brief von einem Mädchen, das sich mit mir in der runden Cocktail-Bar im Palast der Republik treffen wollte. Sie war vorgeschickt worden, um mich auszuhorchen und herauszufinden, ob ich von der Stasi sei. So lernte ich ihren musikbesessenen Freundeskreis kennen, und gemeinsam organisierten wir 1983 ein erstes geheimes Punkkonzert, für das wir die Toten Hosen unauffällig in den Osten schleusten.

Blixa Bargeld had never been to East Berlin. He said what lies beyond the Wall didn't interest him, nor most of the Geniale Dilletanten for that matter. These punks and freaks had come to West Berlin to flee the army, discover themselves and live a life to the max, without limitations. The GDR was real everyday Socialism and it was much too conservative and narrow-minded for most people. It reminded them of the life back home that they had narrowly escaped, and they certainly didn't want to leap out of the frying pan and into the fire. It felt like a much safer habitat living in the shadow of the Berlin Wall.

I on the other hand went to East Berlin very often, not only together with my friend Alistair, Joy Division and New Order, John Peel or my parents, but mainly on my own. I would meet my circle of friends and bring them tapes of the kind of music I was currently listening to. Smuggling music cassettes that I had recorded for them was not in itself very dangerous, but the penalty if I got caught was extremely high. If I had been discovered smuggling, they would have banned me from entering the GDR and that was a price I simply couldn't afford to pay.

I found East Berlin gloriously shabby, in a fascinating way. In winter, it stank of disgusting brown coal, and everywhere hung the stench of pathetic two-stroke petrol engines. It seemed to me, a bit like a parallel world from a *Star Trek* episode, but moreover it was my Disneyland - Disneyland for depressives, and I loved it.

On one of my first visits to East Berlin, I saw a young lad on the Underground train. He had slightly spikey hair and drainpipe trousers but otherwise, he was *normally* dressed. I leapt off the train, stopped him and eagerly questioned him about the possibility of any forthcoming punk concerts in East Berlin. He just stared at me and merely shrugged his shoulders and muttered "There is nothing like that here… it's forbidden!" I couldn't really believe that, so I gave him my address and asked him to send me a postcard if he ever heard of anything. A few months later, I received a letter from a girl called Kerstin, who said she wanted to meet me at the round cocktail bar in the *Palace der Republic* - the East german Parliament building. I thought she had probably been sent to question me, to see if I was perhaps a plant

▶ Mark Reeder vor dem Brandenburger Tor

ist W.
die Klit
der DDR

Ihren Manager Jochen Hülder kannte ich von einem Konzert mit den Einstürzenden Neubauten, Malaria! und Andreas Dorau, das er in der Zeche Bochum veranstaltet hatte. Er hatte damals noch lange Haare gehabt, immer eine Pilotenbrille, eine Bomberjacke und Jeans getragen und war total süchtig nach Coca-Cola gewesen — im Kofferraum seines Autos hatte er stets einen Kasten davon, und Auto gefahren war er nur mit einer Flasche zwischen den Beinen. Er war aber sehr engagiert und hatte einen großartigen Humor.

Campino hatte damals noch bei ZK gesungen und uns gefahren. Er hatte mir erzählt, dass er eine neue Band gründen wolle, die Toten Hosen, ihr Bassist Andi Meurer aber wehrpflichtig sei. Andi zog dann bei mir in einem Kreuzberger Hinterhof als Untermieter ein, um der Bundeswehr zu entgehen. Natürlich nur auf dem Papier, denn meine Ein-Zimmer-Wohnung war gerade mal 21 qm groß, hatte einen Kohleofen, eine Außentoilette und nicht mal heißes Wasser.

In ihren Anfangstagen trieben sich die Toten Hosen sehr oft in Berlin rum. In der Potsdamer Straße gab es damals einen riesigen Ramschladen, der hässliche Siebzigerjahre-Schlaghosen und andere Klamotten aus Pakistan zum Kilopreis verkaufte. Dort kleideten sie sich ein, bevor sie erstmals vor dem Scheißladen in Kreuzberg auftraten, in dem der Deutscheste aller Deutschen, der wahre Heino, Indie-Schallplatten, Import-Scheiben, Musikcassetten und Bootlegs verkaufte und ich gelegentlich als Urlaubsvertretung für ihn einsprang.

Als der wahre Heino dann in ihrem Vorprogramm auftrat, wurde er von einem Doppelgänger, der Volksmusik machte, verklagt. Das Landgericht Bonn entzog ihm das Existenzrecht und verdonnerte ihn zu einer Geldstrafe in Höhe von 10.000 D-Mark. Um die Prozesskosten bezahlen zu können, gaben die Toten Hosen ein Solidaritätskonzert, auf dem der wahre Heino als Kunstfurzer Norbert Hähnel auftrat. Das aufgeblähte Musikstück „Dem Deutschen sein Leid" seines vorerst letzten Auftritts hatte ich produziert, und auch die Fürze stammten von mir. Das Geld kam schließlich zusammen, doch der wahre Heino gab die Kohle lieber aus und saß die Strafe 20 Tage lang im Gefängnis ab.

from the East German Secret Police – the dreaded STASI. This is how I came to know her and her music-obsessed circle of friends. In 1983, we organised the first secret Toten Hosen punk concert together in the East.

I knew their manager, Jochen Hülder, from a concert that he had organised at Zeche, a huge concert venue in Bochum, with Einstürzende Neubauten, Malaria! and Andreas Dorau. Back then, Jochen still had long hair, wore pilot sunglasses, a green bomber jacket and jeans, and he was completely addicted to Coca-Cola. He always had a case of the stuff stashed in the back of his car and he would always drive with a bottle clamped between his legs. But he was very dedicated and had a fantastic sense of humour.

When I first met Campino, he had recently finished with his punkband ZK and he had been designated by Jochen to be my driver for this Zeche concert. I really liked him. He told me that he had just started a new group, the Toten Hosen, but that their bassist, Andi Meurer, was facing compulsory military service. So to avoid being drafted, Andi moved to Berlin, and into my shabby, little Kreuzberger *hinterhof* flat. Officially on paper, he became my flat-mate, but in reality if the authorities had checked my papers, they would have seen we were living together in a tiny 21 square meter, one room flat, which basically had just enough space for one person to live in, let alone two.

In their early days, the Toten Hosen actually spent a lot of time in Berlin. At the top end of Potsdamer Strasse, Andi had discovered a huge clothes shop that sold hideous high waisted flares from the seventies, these ugly bell-bottom trousers came from Pakistan, where even there they had gone out of fashion. This store sold its wares by the kilo. Here, the Hosen bought their unique stage outfits. When in Berlin, it was obligatory for the Hosen to visit Scheissladen in Kreuzberg, where the Germanest, German of all Germans, the *true* Heino, sold indie-records, imports, music cassettes and bootlegs.

The true Heino performed a parody of German folks music hits before every Toten Hosen gig. It was all in good fun. Unfortunately, during a tour with the Hosen, the true Heino was sued by his doppelgänger - the other Heino, who actually made the said German folks music and with it, he

◀ Mark Reeder in NVA-Uniform

Bei einem meiner Besuche des Ostteils der Stadt hatte ich zufällig einen Hippie in einer Kneipe kennengelernt, der angeblich eine Fender Stratocaster besaß — was in der DDR äußerst selten vorkam, da man als Bürger der DDR nicht einfach eine elektrische Gitarre in einem Geschäft kaufen konnte und es dort ohnehin keine Fender-Gitarren gab. Die Produktion von E-Gitarren gehörte eben nicht zum Fünfjahresplan. Der Hippie-Typ erzählte mir jedenfalls, dass in einer Kirche in Rummelsburg jeden Monat eine sogenannte „Blues-Messe" stattfinde. Dieser Gottesdienst, bei dem Songs von Bob Dylan und Eric Clapton gespielt wurden, war eine Form des stillen Protestes gegen das kommunistische System und wurde sogar vom DDR-Regime mehr oder minder geduldet, obwohl die Behörden alles kontrollierten. Allein wer ein Nietenarmband trug, durfte nicht auf dem Alexanderplatz herumlungern und konnte mit einem Platzverbot rechnen, weil das der Vorzeigeplatz der DDR war. Punk Rock ließ sich aber nicht kontrollieren, und die Punks trafen sich immer am Stadtrand, wo sie von den Behörden halbwegs in Ruhe gelassen wurden.

Eigentlich wollte ich selbst mit meiner Band Die Unbekannten in Rummelsburg auftreten, da es in der DDR aber keine Synthesizer und Tonbandgeräte gab, die sich meine Ost-Berliner Freunde Jackie und Kerstin ausborgen konnten, kam nur eine Band infrage, die auf herkömmlichen Instrumenten spielte — die Toten Hosen. Für ihren ersten illegalen Auftritt in der Rummelsburger Erlöserkirche im März 1983 wurden folglich Instrumente und ein Mikrofon von den Bands Feeling B und Planlos zusammengekratzt. Es gab nur einen Verstärker, den die offiziell für den Abend angemeldete Band Planlos zur Verfügung stellte, in der der spätere *Tatort*-Kommissar Bernd Michael Lade Schlagzeug spielte. Wir trafen uns in West-Berlin an der U-Bahn und fuhren in Dreiergruppen in den Osten, wo wir nachmittags mit DDR-Punks Kaffee tranken und Käsekuchen aßen. An jenem Nachmittag lief zufällig ein Bericht über die Toten Hosen und BAP im Westfernsehen, und die Ost-Kids konnten es gar nicht fassen, dass sie gemeinsam mit den Hosen in ihrem Wohnzimmer saßen und sich die Sendung ansahen.

also showed that he had absolutely no sense of humour. The district court in Bonn forbid the true Heino from making any more public appearances as the true Heino and then added a neat little fine of 10 000 Deutsch Marks to sweeten the sentence. In order to pay the legal fees, the Toten Hosen gave a benefit concert for their friend the true Heino, who appeared onstage at the end, as the arthritic father, Norbert Hähnel. For this special event, the true Heino asked me to record and produce a version of the German National Anthem, complete with disgusting farting noises. This flatulent piece of music was to be one of his last performances. In the end, the Hosen managed to collect the money that was needed, but the true Heino gave the money away and decided to sit out the 20 day sentence in jail.

On one of my visits into the eastern part of the city, I fortuitously got to know a hippie in a pub, who claimed to own a real Fender Stratocaster, which in the GDR was extraordinarily rare, since GDR citizens couldn't just buy an electric guitar in a shop and form a band. Besides, there simply weren't any *Fender* guitars to be found. The production of electric guitars wasn't part of the East German five year plan. The hippie told me, that each month in Rummelsburg there was a so-called "blues mass". This was indeed a church service, where songs by such blues greats as Bob Dylan and Eric Clapton were supposedly performed. The institution of the Church in the GDR, was a form of silent protest against the communist system, but regardless of its resistance movement character, it was more or less tolerated by the GDR regime, although everything was monitored by the STASI. Being a punk in the East was very hard, looking like a punk was even harder. Someone merely wearing a studded punky looking armband could be dragged off and imprisoned for practically no reason other than wearing a new wave armband and they could also count on being banned from the Alexander Platz too, because that was the main showplace of the GDR. Punk rock however, tried to resist the STASI monitoring, and most Eastie punks met on the outskirts of the city, away from prying western eyes and where they were usually left in peace.

In reality, I wanted to perform at this Blues Mass in Rummelsburg with my own band, Die Unbekannten, but

▶ Der wahre Heino

Zu dem Zeitpunkt wusste ich noch nicht, dass es das erste Konzert einer West-Band überhaupt war, das illegal in der DDR stattfand. Im DDR-Fernsehen waren zwar schon Bands aus dem Westen aufgetreten, aber dabei hatte es sich um Trash-Pop-Gruppen wie Boney M oder Dschinghis Khan gehandelt. Dass eine echte Punk-Band aus Düsseldorf im Gemeindehaus einer Kirche in Ost-Berlin spielte, war hingegen eine absolute Premiere. Und dabei war jedem klar, dass die Stasi jederzeit zur Tür hereinkommen und uns alle verhaften konnte. Das war Adrenalin pur. Die Anspannung war körperlich zu spüren, und als die Toten Hosen schließlich auftraten, kamen mir die Tränen. Ich konnte kaum glauben, dass wir es tatsächlich geschafft hatten, die Hardcore-Stalinisten auszutricksen. Mehr als das Konzert selbst zählte denn auch, dass die DDR-Punks dadurch ermutigt wurden, selbst Bands zu gründen und sich nicht unterkriegen zu lassen.

Weil ich bereits Malaria! gemixt und als technischer Berater mit Andi in London die Hosen-Single „Bommerlunder" geschnitten hatte, war ich der Live-Mixer der Toten Hosen geworden. (Als die Single veröffentlicht wurde, hatte ich in Jochen Hülders Wohnung kleine Bommerlunder-Fläschchen eingetütet, die der Single beigelegt wurden.) Wir gingen auf eine elendig lange Deutschland-Tournee und ich lernte Orte kennen, die nicht mal Straßennamen hatten.

Bei einem Konzert in Wien schwärmte ich Jochen vor, wie toll es in Budapest sei, und kurzentschlossen fuhren wir beide in die ungarische Hauptstadt und arrangierten einen Auftritt im Young Artists Club mit meinem Freund, dem Fotografen Janos Veto. Die Anreise war allerdings etwas schwierig: Unsere alte Gangster-Limousine, ein verrosteter, urinalweißer Citroen DS, war so schwer beladen, dass das Heck fast auf der Straße hing, und weil die Tankpumpe vorne lag, zeigte die Tankuhr immer an, dass er leer sei, sodass wir fast stündlich anhielten, um zu tanken. Mitten auf der tristen Transitstrecke ging uns dann wirklich das Benzin aus und wir standen hilflos in der Pampa. Ein Österreicher, der mit seinem Wohnwagen vorbeikam, verkaufte uns schließlich einen Liter Sprit für 50 D-Mark, sodass wir weiterfahren konnten — um

◀ Der wahre Heino

since there were no synthesizers or available tape recorders that my East Berlin friends Jackie and Kerstin could borrow for the gig, we had to rethink our strategy. Only one band came into consideration: the Toten Hosen. For their first illegal concert in the Rummelsburger Erlöserkirche in March 1983, we borrowed some instruments and a microphone from the punk bands Planlos and Feeling B. Planlos had registered the gig with the church and we basically hi-jacked it. There was only one amp and that belonged to Planlos, a band in which the future *Tatort* TV Police Commissioner, Bernd Michael Lade, played the drums.

To ensure a successful crossing into the East, we first met in West Berlin at the Underground station and rode over into the East in little inconspicuous groups of three. During the afternoon, we met up with my Eastie friends and all went to their home to drink Ersatzkaffee and eat home-made cheesecake. That afternoon, a report about the Toten Hosen vs. BAP was appearing on West German television. The kids from the East could hardly believe their eyes, actually sitting with the Toten Hosen in their very own living room, watching the TV programme together.

At that time, I didn't know that the gig was the first punk concert by a West German band ever to be held illegally in the GDR. Of course, there had been appearances of western artists on GDR television before but those were trashy pop groups like Boney M, Modern Talking or Dschinghis Khan. That a punk band from Düsseldorf would perform in the parish hall of a church in East Berlin was an absolute first. It was clear to everyone there, that the STASI could break down the door at any moment and arrest everyone. This thought assured for waves of pure adrenaline. You could feel the tension in the air, and as the Toten Hosen finally stepped on the little stage, the tears welled up in my eyes. I could hardly believe that we had managed to pull it off and outsmart the hardcore Stalinist system. More was at stake than just the concert itself, since the GDR punks were emboldened and inspired to start their own groups throughout the entire republic.

I was already the live sound engineer for Malaria! and Jochen trusted my judgement in sound. So I became the technical advisor for Andi in London, where we cut the first

festzustellen, dass sich die nächste Tankstelle nur zwei Minuten entfernt befand. Dem Tankwart fiel dann der Tankverschluss auch noch in einen kleinen Hohlraum zwischen dem Hinterradschutz und der Karosserie, sodass wir das Hinterrad abbauen mussten, um ihn zu bergen. Wir befürchteten, nicht rechtzeitig zu Auftrittsbeginn anzukommen, in der Zwischenzeit hatte es sich aber herumgesprochen, dass deutsche Punk-Bands in dem kleinen Artist Club spielen würden, und das Konzert war in den Kogasz Club der Karl-Marx-Universität verlegt worden. Im Vorprogramm trat ich mit meiner Band Die Unbekannten auf. Als Synthi-Pop-Band waren wir die perfekte Vorgruppe für die Hosen — nach unserem Auftritt konnte es nur besser werden.

Zu dem Konzert waren auch sehr viele besoffene und ziemlich aggressive Redskins gekommen, sogenannte Bunkos, und während die Hosen auf der Bühne standen, klaute jemand unsere Schlagzeugmaschine. Sie wurde uns allerdings großzügig von den Veranstaltern erstattet, und als wir nach dem Konzert Essen gingen, bestellten wir einfach alles, was auf der Karte stand. Vom restlichen Geld kauften wir Lebensmittel für zu Hause und beluden damit den Anhänger; dummerweise verdarb aber ein Großteil, weil unserer Fahrer den Schlüssel des Anhängers abbrach. Auf einer weiteren Hosen-Tournee riss mir nach einer tierisch lauten Rückkopplung das Trommelfell. Der Arzt, den ich konsultierte, fragte mich, ob ich Bauarbeiter sei, und als ich das verneinte und ihm erzählte, dass ich eine Punk-Band mixte, meinte er nur lapidar: „Jetzt nicht mehr." Mit den Toten Hosen hatte ich aber noch einmal zu tun. 1988 organisierte ich gemeinsam mit meinen Freunden aus dem anderen Deutschland einen weiteren Auftritt für sie in Ost-Berlin. Sie sollten auf dem Kinderspielplatz der Hoffnungskirche in Pankow spielen, als Vorgruppe der aus Pankow stammenden DDR-Band Die Vision. Das Ganze war als Benefizkonzert für hungernde rumänische Waisenkinder getarnt, und weil der Pfarrer kurz vor Konzertbeginn die Anweisung erhalten hatte, die Toten Hosen nicht auftreten zu lassen, überredeten wir ihn, die Band als Gruppe aus Dresden anzukündigen. Da ein Auto der Volkspolizei direkt vor der Kirche stand, war klar, dass

Hosen single "Reisefieber". I also became the live sound engineer for the Toten Hosen too. And when their second single *Bommerlunder* was released, I helped to bag the little bottles of Bommerlunder schnapps, which were given away with each single, while staying at Jochen Hülder's flat. I went on incredibly long tours across West Germany with the Hosen and I discovered some places that didn't even have street names.

While attending a Malaria! concert in Vienna with Jochen, I told him how great it was in nearby Budapest. So that night as the Malaria! girls were sleeping, we snook off to the Hungarian capital, to arrange a gig at the Young Artists Club for Die Unbekannten and the Toten Hosen.

For Die Unbekannten, the journey to Budapest was rather demanding. We had engaged the chauffeur services of a french friend with an old gangster limousine, a rusty, urinal-white Citroen DS. It was so heavily loaded down with our equipment, that the back of the car was practically touching the road; and unbeknown to us, because the fuel pump was set forward, the gauge would constantly register empty, so after a few miles, we had to stop to fuel up. Then, whilst driving along the dreary transit route, we actually did run out of petrol, which left us stranded in the middle of nowhere. A nice Austrian samaritan, who was driving by in his caravan, kindly sold us three litres of petrol for 50 Deutsch Marks so we could drive to the next service station – only to find that the next petrol station was two minutes away around the bend ahead in the road. Once there, the dopey petrol station attendant then dropped the petrol tank cap down the little gap between the mudguard and the bodywork, so that we had to dismantle the entire rear end, in order to fish it out. We were afraid that we wouldn't arrive in time for the start of the gig, which in the meantime had been moved to a bigger location, to Kogasz Club at Karl Marx University. My band, Die Unbekannten, was the opening band. As a miserable synthpop band, we were the perfect opener for the Hosen – after us, a gig could only get better. There were a lot of drunk and rather aggressive Red skins, (so-called bunkos) at this exciting gig and while the Hosen were outperforming us, someone managed to steal one of our drum machines. The gig was handsomely paid however, by

▶ Mark Reeder auf dem Ostberliner Alexanderplatz

die DDR-Behörden davon Wind bekommen hatte. Bei einem Blick in die Stasi-Akten nach der Wiedervereinigung kam jedoch heraus, dass eine Informelle Mitarbeiterin offenbar bewusst Informationen zurückgehalten hatte, weil sie selbst die Band hatte sehen wollen. Der Auftritt der Toten Hosen dauerte aber trotzdem nur 45 Minuten, weil irgendein Schlaumeier von der Stasi dahintergekommen war und das Konzert abgebrochen werden musste.

Campino hatte damals gerade stachelige, erdbeerrote Haare und deshalb beim Grenzübergang eine Mütze getragen. Im Suff hatte er sie aber vergessen und bei der Rückkehr nach West-Berlin wurde er am Grenzübergang Friedrichstraße prompt von einem Grenzsoldaten gefragt: „Welcher Idiot hat dich denn reingelassen?" Woraufhin Campino schlagfertig entgegnete: „Einer von euren Idioten." Das fand der jedoch gar nicht lustig, und so wurde Campino abgeführt und mehrere Stunden lang von einem Mann mit einer braunen Nase verhört, bevor man ihn wieder ausreisen ließ.

the organisers, so when we went to eat after the concert, we had so much money, we ordered everything on the menu. From the remaining money, we bought petrol and lots of Hungarian food to bring home to Berlin, which we loaded into our trailer; unfortunately, most of the food ended up spoiled because our driver accidentally broke the key in the lock of the trailer.

During another Toten Hosen tour, I damaged my eardrum after exposure to some really loud feedback. The doctor I consulted asked me if I was a construction worker and when I told him I was the sound engineer for a punk band, he said tersely, "well, not any more."

But I still had one thing to left to do for the Toten Hosen. In 1988, together with my Eastie friends, I helped to organise another secret gig for them in the East part of the city. They were supposed to play at the playground of Hoffnungskirche in Pankow. The opening act was the Pankow-based, Eastie band, Die Vision, who had helped to arrange the gig. The whole thing was disguised as a benefit concert for starving Romanian orphans, but because the pastor, shortly before the start of the concert, had received instructions not to let the Toten Hosen play, we convinced him to present the band as a group from Dresden. It was clear that the GDR authorities had heard about the gig, since there was a Volkspolizei police car, parked directly in front of the church. After reunification, a brief look in the STASI files revealed that an unofficial informer had apparently consciously withheld the information because she wanted to see the band for herself. The performance by the Toten Hosen lasted only for 45 minutes before our deception was discovered and the concert was stopped.

At that time, Campino had spiky strawberry red hair and to cross into the East, he had worn a cap to hide it. Upon the return to West Berlin at the Friedrichstrasse border crossing however, the cap was gone and he was promptly asked by a flabbergasted border guard, "Which idiot let you in?", whereupon Campino cheekily replied, "One of your idiots." The guard didn't find that remark very funny and Campino was hauled off and frog marched to be interrogated for several hours by a dodgy border guard with a brown nose, before he was finally released and allowed to go home.

▶ Zazie de Paris im Film *Der Goldene Oktober*

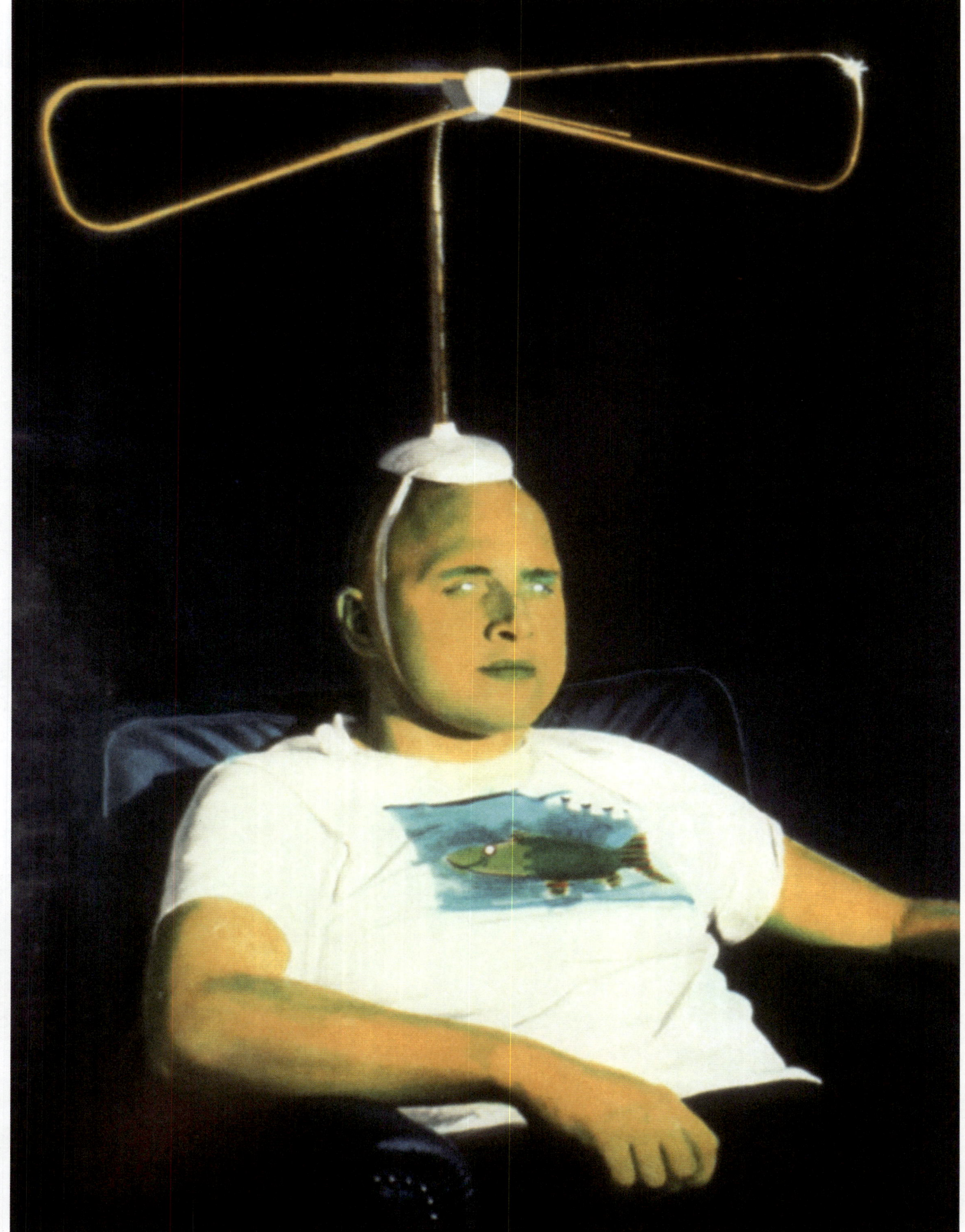

BUM, BUM, BUM

ODER: ES GEHT IMMER WEITER, ALS MAN DENKT

LIFE KEEPS ON GOING LONGER THAN YOU THINK

Ende der Achtzigerjahre waren die geilen Zeiten anscheinend nicht nur für mich vorbei. Der musikalische Underground glich dem Trümmerfeld, das die Randale am 1. Mai 1987 in Kreuzberg hinterlassen hatte. Das Spontane und die radikale Energie waren anscheinend weg. Viele Bands wurden professioneller oder lösten sich auf. Der Ausverkauf des Punk und der Neuen Deutschen Welle hatten zu einem Overkill geführt und die Blase war geplatzt. Clubs und Kneipen wie das SO 36 und das Risiko schlossen ihre Pforten. Die Szene verlor sich im Drogensumpf und leckte ihre Wunden. Oder sie verließ wie Nick Cave die Stadt.

Zum Glück gab es in West-Berlin eine kleine Dance-Szene und ich konnte wenigstens ab und zu in den Ostteil der Stadt flüchten, der mir schon immer abenteuerlicher erschienen war als West-Berlin. Dort konnte man weiterhin sehr radikale Sachen erleben, während die West-Berliner Szene stagnierte.

Meine Gedanken und mein Leben drehten sich jedoch im Kreis. West-Berlin hatte mich verlockt, verschlungen und war nun offensichtlich dabei, mich zu verdauen. Das Frische und Avantgardistische war zu Coffeetable-Musik verkommen, und Radikalität war zur allseits akzeptierten Kunstform geworden. Als ich im Finanzamt eine Beamtin mit hellroten Haarsträhnen sah, dachte ich: Wenn der Underground so sehr in den Mainstream überschwappt, ist alles vorbei. Die Nächte in den Clubs durchzumachen, war keine Lösung mehr. Denn auch die längste Nacht endete irgendwann, und es begann wieder ein Tag, an dem man irgendwie über die Runden kommen musste. Sollte es das wirklich schon gewesen sein?

Es war frustrierend. Der reinste Alptraum. Mein West-Berlin, das seiner Zeit so weit voraus gewesen war, wurde von der Geschichte eingeholt. US-Präsident Ronald Reagan forderte den sowjetischen Präsidenten Michael Gorbatschow auf, die Mauer abzureißen, und im Juni 1987 kam es in Ost-Berlin zu einer „verstärkten Ansammlung dekadent aussehender Jugendlicher", wie es in den DDR-Nachrichten hieß, die einem Konzert von David Bowie vor dem Reichstag im anderen Teil der Stadt lauschen wollten. Zwei Jahre später bröckelte die Mauer endlich und

Towards the end of the eighties, it appeared that the wilder times were obviously over. The musical underground resembled a battlefield. The spontaneous and radical energy was apparently gone. Many bands had either turned professional, or had broken up. The sell-out of punk and German New Wave had led to an overkill and the bubble had finally burst. Bars and Clubs like the SO36 and the Risiko closed their doors. The scene seemed to be sinking into a drug-induced stupor, many fell victim and others, like Nick Cave, realised the party was over and simply left the city. But not for me.

Luckily, in West Berlin, I found sojourn in the small parallel dance scene, which I was already a part of, and if I was ever bored, I would simply flee over into the Eastern part of the city, which I always found to be quite an adventure. I discovered I could still live my life in a fairly radical way, even while the West Berlin scene stagnated.

My life and thoughts were in a bit of a turmoil. West Berlin had tempted me, swallowed me, and was now about to digest me, I didn't want to imagine what came next. The new and avant-garde had degenerated into coffee table music, while radicalism was accepted everywhere as a form of art. When I saw an aging civil servant at the local tax office wearing crimson red hair streaks, I thought, if the radical underground has been absorbed into the mainstream, then it's obviously all over. Spending all night in the clubs wasn't the answer, because, even the longest night came to an end, and another day would begin where one had to make ends meet. Was that all that was left? A nine till five job?

It was very frustrating. Perhaps the worst nightmare. My West Berlin, that had been so ahead of its time was sudenly overtaken by history. U.S. President Ronald Reagan challenged the President of the USSR, Michael Gorbachov, to tear down the Wall. In June 1987, "an intense crowd of decadent looking youths", the GDR news reported, "came to to the border area." They came to hear David Bowie play a concert, directly in front of the Reichstag. On the other side of the city hundreds of fans tried to hear his performance. Two years later, the notorious Berlin Wall finally crumbled and David Hasselhoff was seriously

189-195: SO 36 – das Ende vom Lied

TOD DE
S.O.36

ÜBERHAUPT

TOT

David Hasselhoff brachte sie mit seinem Hit „Looking For Freedom" schließlich zum Einsturz. Zumindest glaubte er das selbst.

Ich verpasste diesen historischen Moment, weil ich in der Nacht vom 8. auf den 9. November 1989 Berlin verließ, um in Ceaucescus Rumänien auf Tournee zu gehen. Wer dachte, nun sei alles vorbei, täuschte sich allerdings. Ein junger DJ namens WestBam alias Westfalia Bambaata alias Maximilian Lenz hatte bereits Mitte der Achtzigerjahre angefangen, im Anschluss an Konzerte im Loft Platten aufzulegen. Nachdem der DJ des Metropol, Chris, seinen Job hingeworfen hatte, suchte der Besitzer Jacques Ihle krampfhaft einen neuen Hi-NRG-DJ. Als Türsteher des Loft und regelmäßiger Besucher des Metropol wurde ich gefragt, ob mir jemand einfiele, und ich schlug ihm WestBam vor. Ihle war allerdings skeptisch, ob so ein junger DJ das Publikum zum Feiern bringen könnte. So musste ich Jacques mühsam überzeugen, indem ich ihn mit Hoodinis – Wodka mit einem Schuss Bitter Lemon – abfüllte, bis er schließlich volltrunken kapitulierte.

WestBam wurde schnell zum Liebling der Berliner Schwulen-Disco-Szene. Es dauerte nicht lange, und er verkündete in einem Essay, dass der DJ schon bald den Platz eines Rockstars einnehmen würde. Er prophezeite eine DJ-Revolution und nannte sie Record Art.

DJs waren nicht länger nur Leute, die Platten auflegten, sondern wurden selbst Popstars. Und Record Art wurde zur neuen Kunstform. In Zirkuszelten veranstaltete WestBam unter dem Motto *Die Macht der Nacht* krasse Partys, auf denen er den Sound der Neubauten-Ära mit House verband.

Beschleunigt wurde diese Entwicklung durch immer bessere Computer und Sequencer, die auf den Markt kamen und von jedermann leicht zu programmieren waren. Die Tracks wurden härter, aber auch melodischer und tanzbarer. Sogar meine Freundin Gudrun Gut war plötzlich von WestBams „Bum Bum Boris" infiziert und es knisterte überall. Was sich nun in den Clubs abspielte, war die Fortsetzung des Punk mit elektronischen Mitteln. Die Berliner Nacht rief wieder laut nach ihren Kindern, die fortan Raver hießen, und man spürte es förmlich, dass

claiming that he had brought it to collapse with his hit "Looking for Freedom". Well, at least that's what he thought. I actually missed this monumental historical moment, because I had left Berlin in the night of 8th to the 9th of November 1989, to go on a tour to Ceaucescu's Romania. Those who thought everything was over were mistaken. The young DJ WestBam, a.k.a. Westfalia Bambaata a.k.a. Maximilian Lenz, had already started to DJ in the middle of the eighties, usually at the end of concerts at Loft. After the main Metropol DJ, Chris, packed in his job, the new owner Jacques Ihle was desperately looking for a new Hi-NRG DJ. As I was the bouncer at Loft and a regular at Metropol, Jaques asked me if I knew any DJs and I suggested WestBam. Ihle was rather sceptical that such a young DJ could get the audience to party. So I had to convince him, which I managed to do by gettig him pissed on his favourite drink, Houdini's – a mixture of vodka and bitter lemon – until, completely inebriated, he finally capitulated.

WestBam soon became the darling of the Berlin gay disco scene and it didn't take long, before he announced in an essay that the DJ would soon take the place of the rockstar. He prophesied a DJ revolution and he called it Record Art. DJs were no longer people who put on records, but they had the potential to become popstars themselves. And Record Art was the new art form. In a huge circus tent, WestBam organised a crazy party, called *The Power of the Night*, in which he combined the sound of the Neubauten era with House music. This development was accelerated by increasingly better computers and sequencers appearing on the market that apparently anyone could easily program. The tracks became harder and faster, but also more melodic and danceable. Even my friend Gudrun Gut was taken by WestBams "Bum Bum Boris" and it crackled everywhere. What was now playing in the clubs was the electronic continuation of punk. The Berlin nightlife called out loudly to her children of the night, who were now known as ravers, and you could feel it in your bones, that something new, something different, something wild was emerging: Acid-House.

◀ David Hasselhoff bringt die Mauer zum Einsturz

198-199: WestBam (rechts) im Studio

wieder etwas Neues, etwas Geiles entstand — Acid-House. Der erste Laden, in dem dieser neue Sound gespielt wurde, war das UFO, ein muffiger, vernebelter Kartoffelkeller einer Wohnung in der Köpenicker Straße. Dimitri Hegemann ließ einfach ein Loch in den Wohnzimmerboden schneiden und eine Treppe einbauen, die in den Keller darunter führte. Fehlten nur noch eine Nebelmaschine und eine Stroboskop-Lampe, und fertig war der Laden. Das UFO war eine Keimzelle im wahrsten Sinne des Wortes. Von der niedrigen Decke hingen Spinnweben, und im Stroboskop-Nebel lief man ständig gegen die Wand; jedes Mal, wenn ich aus dem Laden rauskam, waren meine Klamotten so staubig wie die eines Bauarbeiters — weshalb ich fortan einen Blaumann trug, wenn ich den Club besuchte. Es gab eine eigene leuchtende Biermarke, „Space Bier" — eine andere hätte man in der Dunkelheit, die in dem Club herrschte, sowieso nicht erkannt. Und dort probierte ich zum ersten Mal Ecstacy, was einen gravierenden Einfluss auf meine musikalische Entwicklung hatte.

Eines Abends stand ich vor dem Metropol, als Dr. Motte zu mir kam und mir von einer Demo erzählte, die am 1. Juli 1989 stattfinden sollte. Mit theatralischen Gesten gab er mir zu verstehen, dass die Demo sich nicht gegen etwas richten solle, sondern für etwas: die Liebe. Ich fand das großartig und war sofort dabei.

An jenem Samstagnachmittag verwandelten knapp 150 Raver den Kudamm in einen Dancefloor. Unter dem Motto „Friede, Freude, Eierkuchen" demonstrierten wir für Liebe und Freiheit, doch Dr. Motte, einer der Erfinder dieser *Love Parade*, ahnte genauso wenig wie wir, dass ein paar Jahre später über eine Million Techno-Fans aus aller Welt zu diesem Mega-Event strömen würden. WestBams Karriere nahm dadurch jedenfalls mächtig Fahrt auf und er hatte schon bald seinen eigenen Truck auf der *Love Parade* und komponierte jedes Jahr eine neue Hymne für sie.

Auch ich ahnte an diesem regnerischen Samstagnachmittag nicht, dass dieser Aufruf zu mehr Freiheit nicht unerhört bleiben würde und welche dramatischen Konsequenzen er nach sich ziehen sollte, die Berlin und die Welt total veränderten.

Am 9. November 1989 fiel die Mauer und die Techno-Bewegung wurde dadurch immer stärker. Die elektronische

The first place where this new sound could be heard was the UFO club, a mouldy, dusty old potato cellar in a flat on Köpenicker Strasse. Dimitri Hegemann simply cut a big hole in the living room floorboards, built in some steps that led to the cellar and installed a soundsystem. He just needed a fog maschine and a strobe lamp and he was all set. The UFO was a germ cell in the truest sense of the word. Spiderwebs hung from the low ceiling, and in the strobe highlighted fog, you would regularly bump into the wall; every time I came out of that place, my clothes were disgracefully dusty and looked like a construction worker's – which is why I decided to start wearing German electricians Blue working suits, whenever I visited the club. Dimitri had even created his own luminiscent beer brand, "Space Beer". It was here that I first tried Ecstasy, which definitely had a serious influence on my later musical development.

One evening, I was standing in front of the Metropol when Dr. Motte came up to me and told me about a demonstration that was due to take place the following weekend on July 1st 1989. With theatrical gestures, he let me know that the demonstration was not against something but *for* something: Love! I thought, that's brilliant. Finally a demonstration that is *for* something.

On that rainy Saturday afternoon about 150 ravers transformed the Kudamm into a dance floor. Under the motto, "Peace, Happiness and Pancakes", we demonstrated for love, peace and freedom, although Dr. Motte, one of the originators of this *Love Parade,* had little notion as any of us did, that a few years later, almost two million techno fans, from all over the world would be pouring into Berlin for this mega-event. WestBam's career also took off and he soon had his own float on the Love Parade, for which he composed a new hymn every year.

I also had no idea on that soaking Saturday afternoon that our call for freedom would not go unheard, nor what the dramatic consequences would be following an event that would change Berlin and the whole world forever.

On the 9th November 1989, the Berlin Wall came down, and with it, the techno movement grew instantly stronger. The search for electronic music that had initially drawn

▶▲ WestBam

Musik, die mich zehn Jahre zuvor von Manchester nach West-Berlin gelockt hatte, ließ nun auch meinen Traum wahr werden: Ich gründete das erste Trance-Label überhaupt und nannte es MFS. Ursprünglich war das die Abkürzung für das Ministerium für Staatssicherheit, also die Stasi, nun aber stand sie für Masterminded For Success. Mit der Ost-Berliner Gruppe Die Vision hatte ich noch vor dem Mauerfall für Amiga, die staatliche Plattenfirma der DDR, das letzte Album produziert, das im kommunistischen Teil der Stadt aufgenommen wurde. Dass ausgerechnet mir als Engländer diese Ehre zuteil wurde, war mir damals nicht bewusst, aber so lernte ich die Leute von Amiga kennen und konnte nach dem Mauerfall ihre Räumlichkeiten und ihre Infrastruktur nutzen, um mein Label zu starten, das sich als Plattform für junge Künstler aus der DDR verstand.

Heute kennen die Kids nur noch Casting Shows und glauben, man müsse zigtausend Likes haben, um eine gewisse Akzeptanz zu erreichen. Als ich nach Berlin kam, gab es aber noch keine Handys oder Facebook und man musste in einen Club gehen, um mit seinen Freunden zu kommunizieren. Die Lebensbedingungen waren damals viel extremer, es gab kaum Zentralheizungen, sondern meist Kohleöfen, und man ging nicht zuletzt auch in einen Club, weil es dort im Winter wenigstens warm war. Ja, so war das damals im wilden West-Berlin der Achtzigerjahre. Mitten im Kalten Krieg haben wir mit Symbolen gespielt, mit Gesetzen und Uniformen, mit Musik, Steinen und Scherben. Wir haben kaputt gemacht, was kaputt zu machen war, Tabus gebrochen, Grenzen überschritten, Utopien verwirklicht und uns genommen, was wir wollten. Wir haben Geschichte erlebt und auch geschrieben.

Letztlich sind die Achtzigerjahre aber wie im Flug vergangen und West-Berlin ist Geschichte. Eine, zugegeben, ziemlich wahnsinnige Geschichte, aus der ich eins gelernt habe: Es geht immer weiter, als man denkt. Man muss einfach nur etwas machen.

Vielleicht inspiriert meine Geschichte von Berlin ja den einen oder anderen Leser, den nächsten Schritt zu tun. Ich bin jedenfalls froh, dass ich ihn gemacht habe, und kann zurecht sagen: Ich war dabei, und es war sehr, sehr geil.

me from Manchester to West Berlin, was now a reality: I founded the first Trance label and called it MFS. Originally, this was the abbreviation for the Ministry of State security - the STASI, but from now on it would mean; *Masterminded for Success.* This idea would certainly never have come to me before the Wall fell. I had been producing an album in East berlin with the group Die Vision, and it would become the last album recorded in communist East Germany, for the state owned record company, Amiga. That this honour was accorded to me, an Englishman, was at that time a mystery to me, but at least I got to know the people at Amiga, and after the fall of the Wall I was able to use their office space and infrastructure to start my own label, which I saw as a platform for hopeful young artists from the former GDR.

Today, kids only know casting shows and many believe that one has to have a zillion likes to be popular and achieve a certain level of acceptability. When I came to Berlin, there were no mobiles, nor Facebook and you had to go to a club to communicate with your friends. The living conditions back then were much more extreme: there was almost no central heating, but coal ovens, and you went to a club in the winter because it was at least warm there. Yes, that's how it was in the wild West Berlin of the eighties. We were stuck in the middle of the Cold War, we played with symbols, with the law and uniforms, with music, stones and shards. We destroyed things that could be destroyed, we broke taboos, exceeded limits, realised utopias and took what we wanted. We lived history and we also wrote it. Ultimately, the eighties have gone by in a flash and West Berlin is history, a rather frenzied history, from which I discovered one thing: Life keeps going on and on, longer than you think. You just have to do it.

Perhaps my story about West Berlin will inspire others to take the next step. All I can say is that I'm proud I've done it and I can rightly say: I was there and it was all pretty fucking geil!

ZUGABE

DIE MITWIRKENDEN / THE CONTRIBUTORS

▲◀ Grenzübergang Chausseestraße
▲▶ Demo gegen Ronald Reagan am Winterfeldtplatz
▼◀ Die Mauer
▼▶ Bernauer Straße/Wedding

Adrian Wright
Keyboarder der britischen Synthie-Pop-Band The Human League und zuständig für deren visuelle Effekte bei Live-Auftritten.

Alexander Hacke (Alexander von Borsig)
Das „Wunderkind" des Berliner Undergrounds gründete zusammen mit Volker Hauptvogel das Mekkanik Destruktif Kommandöh, war Mitglied der Minimal-Electro-Gruppe P1/E, der Band Flucht nach vorn und — unter dem Namen Alexander von Borsig — Gitarrist der Einstürzenden Neubauten.

Alistair Gray
Aus England stammender Wahlberliner und Sänger von Die Unbekannten und später Shark Vegas.

Andi Meurer
Mitbegründer und Bassist der Düsseldorfer Punkband Die Toten Hosen.

Anita Lane
Australische Sängerin, die nicht nur mit Nick Cave liiert war, sondern mit ihm auch Songs für dessen Bands The Birthday Party und The Bad Seeds schrieb. Nach der Trennung von Cave lebte sie vorübergehend mit dem Spex-Autor Oliver Schund zusammen und nahm u.a. eine Cover-Version des italienischen Partisanenliedes „Bella Ciao" auf, das auch im Film *Herr Lehmann* zu hören ist.

Annette Humpe
1950 in Hagen geboren, sang sie zunächst mit ihrer Schwester Inga bei den Neonbabies, bevor sie Ideal gründete. Nach der Trennung von Ideal veröffentlichte sie mit ihrer Schwester Inga den DÖF-Hit „Codo" und unter dem Namen Humpe & Humpe zwei Alben. Seither betätigt sie sich äußerst erfolgreich als Songschreiberin und Produzentin u.a. für Heiner Pudelko, Udo Lindenberg, Die Prinzen, Rio Reiser, Ich + Ich und Max Raabe.

Keyboardist for the British synthpop band The Human League and responsible for their visual effects for live performances.

Berlin Underground "Wunderkind" who founded, along with Volker Hauptvogel, the Mekkanik Destruktif Kommandöh, and was also a member of the Minimal Electro group P1/E, the band Flucht nach vorn and — under the name Alexander von Borsig — guitarist for the Einstürzende Neubauten.

Originally from England but a native of Berlin by choice, singer for Die Unbekannten and later Shark Vegas.

Co-founder and bassist of the Düsseldorf group Die Toten Hosen.

Australian singer, not only in a relationship with Nick Cave but who also wrote songs with him for his bands The Birthday Party and The Bad Seeds. After she split up with Cave, she lived for a while with the Spex author Oliver Schund, and recorded, amongst other things, a cover for the Italian partisan song "Bella Ciao" that can be heard in the film Herr Lehmann.

Born in Hagen in 1950, she, along with her sister Inga, sang with the Neonbabies before she founded Ideal. After splitting up with Ideal, she and her sister Inga released the DÖF (Deutsch-Österreichisches Feingefühl/German Austrian sensitivity) hit "Codo", as well as two albums under the name Humpe & Humpe. Since then, she has worked successfully as a songwrite and producer for, amongst others, Heiner Pudelko, Udo Lindenberg, Die Prinzen, Rio Reiser, Ich + Ich and Max Raabe.

Bernard Sumner

Gitarrist und Keyboarder von Joy Division. Sänger und Gitarrist von New Order, Electronic und Bad Lieutenant.

Guitarist and keyboardist for Joy Division. Singer and guitarist for New Order, Electronic and Bad Lieutenant.

Bettina Köster

1959 in Herford geboren, studierte sie an der Berliner Hochschule für Künste, bevor sie bei DIN A Testbild, Mania D, Liebesgier und Malaria! sang und Saxophon spielte.

Born in Herford in 1959, she studied at the Berlin University for the Arts before she became a singer and saxophone player for DIN A Testbild, Mania D, Liebesgier and Malaria!.

Blixa Bargeld

1959 als Christian Emmerich in Berlin geboren. Genialer Dilletant, Gründer der Einstürzenden Neubauten und Gitarrist von Nick Cave and The Bad Seeds, die 1987 auch in Wim Wenders' Spielfilm Der Himmel über Berlin mitspielten.

Born in Berlin in 1959 as Christian Emmerich. One of the Geniale Dilletanten, founder of the Einstürzende Neubauten und guitarist for Nick Cave and The Bad Seeds, he also appeared in Wim Wenders' 1987 film Der Himmel über Berlin.

Campino

1962 als Andreas Frege in Düsseldorf geboren. Sänger der Punkbands ZK und Die Toten Hosen. Lebt in Düsseldorf und Berlin.

Born in Düsseldorf in 1962 as Andreas Frege. Singer for the punk bands ZK and Die Toten Hosen. He lives in Düsseldorf and Berlin.

Carlo Karges (1951 – 2002)

Gründungsmitglied von Novalis und Gitarrist von Tomorrow's Gift, dem Release Music Orchestra, den Hagener Bands The Ramblers und Extrabreit und von Nena. Komponist von „99 Luftballons". Verstarb 2002 an Leberversagen.

Founding member of Novalis as well as guitarist for Tomorrow's Gift, the Release Music Orchestra, and the Hagen bands The Ramblers and Extrabreit, and for Nena. Composer of "99 Luftballons". Died in 2002 from liver failure.

Cassia Hecker (1963 - 1986)

Mitglied der hauseigenen Noise-Band Mannamaschine des Frisörsalons Penny Lane. Nachdem sie angeblich „intimen Kontakt" zu Charles Manson hatte und sich mit Jeanne d'Arc identifizierte, beging sie Selbstmord am Strand ihrer Heimatstadt Cuxhaven, indem sie sich am Faschingsdienstag 1986, nur wenige Monate nach der Geburt ihrer Tochter und mit einer Kette aus Gummibärchen bekleidet, mit Benzin übergoss und anzündete.

Member of the self-developed Noise band Mannamaschine from the hair salon Penny Lane. After she ostensibly had "intimate contact" with Charles Manson, and saw herself to be like Joan of Arc, she committed suicide on the beach near her hometown of Cuxhaven on Mardigras 1986 just a few months after the birth of her daughter; while wearing a necklace of gummy bears, she doused herself with gasoline and set fire to herself.

Notorische Reflexe

Monika Döring

Christiane Felscherinow

Protagonistin des autobiografischen Buchs und Films *Christiane F — Wir Kinder vom Bahnhof Zoo* und Freundin von Alexander Hacke, die auch als Musikerin beim Festival Genialer Dilletanten und Schauspielerin (Neonstadt, Decoder) Aufsehen erregte. Auf einer Promotionreise für ihren Film durch die USA machte sie den Radio-DJ Rodney Bingenheimer auf Nenas „99 Luftballons" aufmerksam, der den Song in seiner Sendung spielte und so der Band zum internationalen Durchbruch verhalf. Auch Klaus Maeck wohnte eine Zeit lang mit ihr zusammen.

Protagonist of the autobiographical book and film Christiane F — Wir Kinder vom Bahnhof Zoo, and girlfriend of Alexander Hacke, she caused a sensation as a musician at the Festival Genialer Dilletanten and as an actress (Neonstadt, Decoder). On a promotion tour through the USA for her film, she introduced the radio DJ Rodney Bingenheimer to Nena's "99 Luftballons"; he then played the song in his broadcast, helping to propel the band to their international breakthrough. She lived for a while together with Klaus Maeck.

Christoph Dreher

1952 in Nürnberg geborener Dokumentarfilm-Regisseur und Mitbegründer der No-Wave-Band Die Haut. Seit 2000 ist Dreher Professor für audiovisuelle Medien an der Merz Akademie für Gestaltung in Stuttgart.

Born in Nürnberg in 1952, documentary film director and co-founder of the No Wave band Die Haut. Since 2000, Dreher is Professor for audiovisual media at the Merz Akademie for Design in Stuttgart.

Claudia Skoda

Nachdem die Modedesignerin 1975 Martin Kippenberger auf Ibiza kennengelernt hatte, veranstaltete sie in ihrer Künstler-WG Fabrikneu in der Zossener Straße in Kreuzberg Modenschauen, auf der sie avantgardistische Strickkonzepte vorstellte, die auch David Bowie und Iggy Pop anzogen.

After she met the fashion designer Martin Kippenberger on Ibiza in 1975, she hosted fashion shows at her artist's commune Fabrikneu on the Zossener Straße in Kreuzberg where she presented avant-garde knitting creations which were worn by people such as David Bowie and Iggy Pop.

David Bowie

Das Chamäleon des Pop wohnte von 1976 bis 1978 in der Schöneberger Hauptstraße 155, nahm in den Hansa-Studios die Alben *Low* und *Heroes* auf und produzierte dort auch Iggy Pops Alben *The Idiot* und *Lust For Life*. Drehte in seiner Berliner Zeit, in der er mit Claudia Skoda, Martin Kippenberger und Romy Haag befreundet war, Marlene Dietrichs letzten Film *Schöner Gigolo, armer Gigolo* und ließ sich nachhaltig vom Expressionismus der Zwanzigerjahre inspirieren. 2013 veröffentlichte er den Song „Where Are We Now", in dem er seine Berliner Zeit verarbeitete.

The chameleon of Pop lived on Schöneberger Hauptstraße 155 from 1976 to 1978, recorded the albums Low and Heroes at the Hansa studios, and also produced Iggy Pop's albums The Idiot und Lust For Life there. During his time in Berlin while friends with Claudia Skoda, Martin Kippenberger and Romy Haag, he also made Marlene Dietrich's last film, Schöner Gigolo, armer Gigolo, inspired by the expressionism of the nineteen-twenties. In 2013, he released the song "Where Are We Now", reflecting on his Berlin years.

Dimitri Hegemann

1954 in Werl geboren, studierte er 1978 an der Freien Universität Musikwissenschaft, bevor er Bassist der New-Wave-Band Leningrad Sandwich wurde, in den Achtzigerjahren Atonal-Festivals für nonkonforme Musik veranstaltete und mit dem Fischbüro einen Raum für vielseitige Experimente betrieb. Hegemanns Ufo-Club war die Keimzelle der Berliner Technoszene und mit dem Tresor eröffnete er 1990 einen der weltweit bekanntesten Techno-Clubs. Seit 2000 betreibt er zusammen mit Ben Becker das Lokal Trompete.

Born in Werl in 1954, he studied at the Free University of Musicology before he became bassist for the New Wave band Leningrad Sandwich, organised atonal festivals for non-conformist music in the eighties, and with Fischbüro operated a space for wide-ranging experiments. Hegemann's UFO club was the nucleus for the Berlin techno scene, and with the Tresor, he opened in 1990 one of the world's most famous techno clubs. Since 2000, he runs the pub Trompete with Ben Becker.

Dr. Motte

Der 1960 in Spandau geborene Techno-DJ Matthias Roeingh initiierte die Love Parade, die er bis 2006 auch organisierte. Wandte sich nach seinem Rückzug gegen die Kommerzialisierung dieser „Tanzbewegung" und der Gegenveranstaltung Fuck Parade zu. Mitbegründer von electrocult, einem Verein zur Förderung und Pflege der elektronischen Musik- und Clubkultur und des damit verbundenen Lebensgefühls.

Born in Spandau in 1960, the techno DJ Matthias Roeingh initiated the Love Parade, which he has also organised since 2006. After his retirement, he turned against the commercialisation of this "dance movement" and the counter-event "Fuck Parade". Co-founder of electrocult, an organisation for the promotion and maintenance of electronic music and club culture, as well as its associated lifestyle.

Edgar Froese (1944 – 2015)

Pionier der elektronischen Musik und Gründer von Tangerine Dream.

Electronic music pioneer and founder of Tangerine Dream.

Elisabeth Recker

Gründete gemeinsam mit Michael Voigt das Monogam-Label und war zeitweilig mit Nick Cave liiert.

Together with Michael Voigt, she founded the Monogam label and was for a time together with Nick Cave.

Gabriele Susanne Kerner (Nena)

1960 in Hagen geborene Sängerin, die Anfang der Achtzigerjahre nach Berlin umzog, in Jim Raketes Fabrik die Fanpost von Spliff beantwortete und schließlich mit bzw. als Nena auch in den USA und England Karriere machte.

Born in Hagen in 1960, moved to Berlin in the beginning of the eighties, worked at Jim Rakete's Fabrik answering fan mail for Spliff, then made her career as Nena with success extending to England and the USA.

Nena

Gudrun Gut

1957 in Celle als Gudrun Bredemann geboren, studierte die Schlagzeugerin und Sängerin, Moderatorin und Produzentin ab 1978 Visuelle Kommunikation an der Berliner Hochschule der Künste. Unter dem Namen Gudrun Gut spielte sie u.a. bei DIN A Testbild, Mania D und Malaria! und gründete gemeinsam mit Blixa Bargeld die Einstürzenden Neubauten. Nachdem sie von 1997 bis 2012 für Radio Eins die Sendung *Ocean Club Radio* moderiert hatte, arbeitet sie heute als DJ und veröffentlicht auf ihrem Label Monika Enterprise regelmäßig auch eigene Tonträger.

Born in Celle in 1957 as Gudrun Bredemann, the drummer, singer, presenter and producer studied visual communication at the Berlin University of the Arts from 1978. Under the name Gudrun Gut, she played with groups including DIN A Testbild, Mania D und Malaria!, and founded the Einstürzende Neubauten together with Blixa Bargeld. After working as a presenter for the Radio Eins broadcast Ocean Club Radio from 1997 to 2012, she now works as a DJ and regularly releases her own recordings on her label Monika Enterprise.

Helga Götze (1922 – 2008)

Aktivistin für sexuelle Befreiung („Ficken ist Frieden"), die auch in Rosa von Praunheims Film *Rote Liebe* zu sehen ist. Vor der Gedächtniskirche und der Mensa der TU Berlin trug sie eine Zeit lang täglich Gedichte vor.

Activist for sexual liberation ("Fucking is Peace"), appearing in Rosa von Praunheim's film Rote Liebe. She recited poems for a period of time in front of the Kaiser Wilhelm Memorial church (Gedächtniskirche) as well as in front of the Technical University Berlin canteen.

Ian Curtis (1956 – 1980)

Sänger und Gitarrist von Warsaw und Joy Division. An Epilepsie erkrankt, litt Curtis zunehmend unter Depressionen, die sich auch in seinen Texten ausdrückten. Nachdem seine Frau die Scheidung eingereicht hatte, erhängte Curtis sich einen Tag vor Beginn einer US-Tournee von Joy Division.

Singer and guitarist for Warsaw and Joy Division. Afflicted with epilepsy, Curtis suffered from depression, which he expressed in his lyrics. After his wife filed for divorce, Curtis hanged himself one day before the start of Joy Division's US tour.

Iggy Pop

Der „Godfather of Punk" lebte von 1967 bis 1978 im selben Haus wie David Bowie, der seine erfolgreichsten Hits „The Passenger" und „Lust For Life" produzierte und ihm zu einem Comeback verhalf.

From 1967 to 1978, the "Godfather of Punk" lived in the same house with David Bowie, who was the producer for his most successful hits "The Passenger" and "Lust for Life" and who helped him make a comeback.

Jim Rakete

Fotograf des allerersten Bandporträts der Kreuzberger Polit-Rockband Ton Steine Scherben und Manager der Nina Hagen Band, von Spliff, Nena und Interzone.

Photographer for the very first band portraits of the Kreuzberg political rock band Ton Steine Scherben, as well as manager of the Nina Hagen band, of Spliff, of Nena, and of Interzone.

Jochen Hülder (1957 – 2015)
Konzertveranstalter, Manager der Toten Hosen und Geschäftsführer des bandeigenen Labels Totenkopf und JKP (Jochens Kleine Plattenfirma). Er betreute auch Malaria!

Concert promoter, manager of the Toten Hosen and managing director of the band's own label Totenkopf and JKP. He also managed Malaria!

Jörg Buttgereit
1963 in Berlin geborener Filmkritiker und Regisseur von Splatter Movies wie *Nekromantik 1 & 2* und *Der Todesking* sowie der Dokumentation *So war das SO 36 — Ein Abend der Nostalgie*. 2005 inszenierte er das Ramones-Musical *Gabba Gabba Hey,* seit 2007 ist er auch als Regisseur für das Berliner Hebbel-Theater und das Schauspiel Dortmund tätig.

Born in Berlin in 1963, film critic and director of splatter films such as Nekromantik 1 & 2 and Der Todesking as well as the documentary So war das SO 36 — Ein Abend der Nostalgie. In 2005, he staged the Ramone's musical Gabba Gabba Hey, and since 2007 he has worked as a director for the Berlin Hebbel Theater and Schauspiel Dortmund.

John Peel (1939 – 2004)
Legendärer englischer Radio-Moderator mit einem außergewöhnlichen Gespür für neue Musik, dessen Sendungen im BBC World Service und auf BFBS sich auch in Deutschland größter Beliebtheit erfreuten und sogar vom DDR-Jugendsender DT 64 übernommen wurden.

Legendary English radio host with an extraordinary instinct for new music, whose broadcasts on the BBC World Service and on BFBS enjoyed great popularity also in Germany, and which were even made part of the GDR youth broadcast DT 64.

Käthe B. (1962 – 2011)
In Eckernförde geborener „Medienhengst", der sich in den Achtzigerjahren Kerzen, Glühbirnen oder Tannenbäume auf die Glatze klebte und damit in Berlin herumlief. Zu den Mitgliedern des 1986 gegründeten Käthe B. Fan Clubs, aus dem man nicht austreten kann, zählen u.a. Madonna und Paul Simon.

Born in Eckernförde, a media jackass who during the eighties would glue candles, lightbulbs or Christmas trees on her shaved head and run around Berlin. The Kathe B. Fan Club which doesn't allow members to resign, was founded in 1986 and includes Madonna and Paul Simon.

Kain Karawahn
1959 in Salzgitter geborener Künstler, der sich in Theorie und Praxis mit der Beziehung des Menschen zum Feuer auseinandersetzt und 1984 zusammen mit Tom Kummer die Mauer in Flammen setzte.

Born in Salzgitter in 1959, an artist who immersed himself in the theory and practice of the Relationship of Mankind to Fire, and who, along with Tom Kummer, in 1984, set the Wall on fire.

Keith Haring (1958 – 1990)
Von Graffiti beeinflusster US-amerikanischer Künstler, der 1986 auch die Mauer am Checkpoint Charlie bemalte.

US American artist influenced by graffiti who also painted the Wall at Checkpoint Charlie in 1986.

▲◀ Schund aka Oliver Schütz
▲▶ Lysanne Thibeaudeau
▼◀ Selfie von Knut Hoffmeister
▼▶ Padeluun

Kiddy Citny

1957 in Stuttgart geboren, bemalte er 1985 die Mauer mit überdimensionalen Köpfen, um „Ost-Berlin mit Kunst einzuschließen". Die Ost-Berliner Firma Limex warf ihm daraufhin „Sachbeschädigung von Grenzeinrichtungen" vor, scheute sich aber nicht, die „Schmierereien" für eine halbe Million D-Mark an das New Yorker Museum of Modern Art (MOMA) zu verkaufen. Ein von Citny bemaltes Mauerstück diente Wim Wenders im Film *Der Himmel über Berlin* als Kulisse, auf dessen Soundtrack Citny auch mit seiner Band Sprung aus den Wolken zu hören ist.

Born in Stuttgart in 1957, painted the Wall in 1985 with oversized heads in order to "enclose East Berlin with art". The East Berlin company Limex accused him of "criminal damage to border facilities" yet, nonetheless, didn't hesitate to sell the "graffiti" for a half a million Deutschmarks to the New York Museum of Modern art (MOMA). One of Citny's painted Wall segments served as the backdrop to Wim Wender's film Der Himmel über Berlin, whose soundtrack features Citny with his band Sprung playing from the clouds.

Klaus Maeck

Gründer des Punk-Plattenladens und -vertriebs Rip Off, Musikverleger, Manager der Einstürzenden Neubauten, langjähriger Produzent des Filmemachers Fatih Akin (u.a. *Soul Kitchen*) und des Films *Fraktus*, Regisseur von *Decoder* und, zusammen mit Jörg A. Hoppe und Heiko Lange, von *B-Movie*.

Founder of the punk record and distribution shop Rip Off, music publisher, manager of the Einstürzende Neubauten, longtime producer for the filmmaker Fatih Akin (including Soul Kitchen) and the film Fraktus, director of Decoder, and together with Jörg A. Hoppe and Heiko Lange, of B-Movie.

Klaus-Jürgen Rattay (1962 – 1981)

In Kleve am Niederrhein geborener Hausbesetzer, der im Zuge der Räumung von acht besetzten Häusern von einem Bus erfasst und zu Tode geschleift wurde.

Born in Kleve on the Niederrhein, a squatter who during the aftermath of evictions from eight occupied houses, was caught up by a bus and dragged to his death.

Knut Hoffmeister

1956 in Peine geborener Multimedia-Künstler und Mitbegründer der Notorischen Reflexe, der u.a. mit Martin Kippenberger und Luciano Castelli (Geile Tiere) zusammenarbeitete.

Born 1956 in Peine. Multimedia Artist and Co-Founder of Notorische Reflexe, who worked with Martin Kippenberger and Luciano Castelli (Geile Tiere).

Lucy Weisshaupt

Einst Inhaberin des Frisörsalons Penny Lane in der Potsdamer Straße 159. Wohnt noch immer dort, auch wenn der Salon heute einer Gartenlaube gleicht.

Once the owner of the hair salon Penny Lane on the Potsdamer Straße 159. Still lives there although the salon now resembles a gazebo.

Martin Kippenberger (1953 – 1997)

In Dortmund geborener Künstler, der zu den Neuen Wilden gezählt wird und Ende der Siebzigerjahre das SO 36 als Geschäftsführer übernahm. Veröffentlichte auf seinem Label S.O. 36 Records die Doppel-Single „Luxus" mit New Yorker Straßengeräuschen.

An artist born in Dortmund, considered part of the New Wild Style (Neue Wilde), became the general manager of the SO 36 at the end of the seventies. Released the double single "Luxus" on his label S.O. 36 Records which incorporated street sounds from New York.

Michael Schäumer

Mitglied des Elektronikprojektes P1/E und Mitbegründer des Labels Exil-System, das seinen Namen Oswald Wieners Restaurant Exil verdankt, in dem Schäumer in der Küche arbeitete.

Member of the electronic project P1/E and co-founder of the label Exil-System, which owes its name to Oswald Wiener's restaurant Exil where Schäumer worked in the kitchen.

Michael Voigt

Gründer des Monogam-Labels, der gemeinsam mit seiner Partnerin Elisabeth Recker auch das Projekt Rainy Day Women auf Vinyl verewigte.

Founder of the Monogam label through which he and his partner Elisabeth Recker immortalised the project Rainy Day Women on vinyl.

Monika Dietl

Wegweisende fränkische Radiomoderatorin, die Ende der Achtzigerjahre vom *Zündfunk* (BR) zum *SFBeat* (SFB) wechselte und in ihren Sendungen verschlüsselte Hinweise auf illegale Techno-Partys gab.

A ground-breaking radio host from Franconia who moved from Zündfunk (BR) to SFBeat (SFB) at the end of the eighties, and who gave encrypted messages about illegal techno parties during her broadcasts.

Monika Döring

Betreiberin der Music Hall und des Loft am Nollendorfplatz und große Förderin Berliner Indie-Bands.

Ran the Music Hall and the Loft at Nollendorfplatz, and was a big patron of Berlin's indie rock bands.

Muriel Gray

Die 1958 geborene Schottin spielte in der Punk-Band The Family Von Trapp, bevor sie für *Time Out*, den *Sunday Herald* und den *Guardian* schrieb, die Channel-4-Show *The Tube* moderierte und 1988 Rektorin der Universität Edinburgh wurde. Autorin des Horror-Romans *The Ancient*.

Born in Scotland in 1958, played in the punk band The Family Von Trapp before she became a writer for Time Out, the Sunday Herald and the Guardian, hosted the Channel 4 show The Tube, and became headmistress at the University of Edinburgh. Author of the horror novel The Ancient.

Nick Cave

Australischer Musiker, Schriftsteller (u.a. Und die Eselin sah den Engel) und Drehbuchautor (u.a. Ghosts ... of the Civil Dead), der von 1983 bis 1986 in West-Berlin lebte, die Stadt aber wieder verließ, als Berlin den Bach runterging, um sich nicht im Drogensumpf zu verlieren.

Australian musician, writer (including Und die Eselin sah den Engel), and screenwriter (including Ghosts… of the Civil Dead), who lived in West Berlin from 1983 to 1986, but left the city as Berlin went down the pan, to avoid burning himself out on drugs.

Nina Hagen

1955 in Ost-Berlin geborene „staatlich geprüfte Schlagersängerin", die im Zuge der Ausbürgerung des Liedermachers Wolf Biermann in den Westen gelangte und sowohl in der DDR (mit dem Lied „Du hast den Farbfilm vergessen") als auch in der BRD (mit der Nina Hagen Band, aber auch solo) erfolgreich war.

Born in East Berlin in 1955, a "diploma-certified pop singer" who arrived in the West around the time the songwriter Wolf Biermann was stripped of his nationality, and who achieved success both in the GDR (with the song "Du hast den Farbfilm vergessen") as well as in the FRG (with the Nina Hagen band as well as a solo artist).

Norbert Hähnel

1951 geborener Fan des Fußballvereins Arminia Bielefeld und Betreiber des Kreuzberger Scheißladens. Besser bekannt als Der wahre Heino.

Born in 1951, a fan of the football club Arminia Bielefeld who ran the Krezberger Scheißladen. Better known as the wahre Heino.

Ratten-Jenny

Als Jenny Schmidt geborene „Künstlerin ohne Werk" und Stammgast des SO 36. Als dessen neuer Besitzer Martin Kippenberger sie „vollkommen grundlos" vor die Tür setzen wollte und sie sich im Gerangel die Hand mit einer Glasscherbe aufschlitzte, schlug sie ihm das restliche Glas ins Gesicht. Einer anderen Version zufolge ereignete sich dieser Vorfall im Café Central, wo Ratten-Jenny von Kippenberger mit dem Ruf „Na, du Fotze!" begrüßt wurde. Die Begegnung mit der anschließend nach London emigrierten Hausbesetzerin inspirierte Kippenberger schließlich zu seinem Bild „Dialog mit der Jugend".

Born as Jenny Schmidt, known as "an artist without portfolio" and a regular at the SO 36. When the new owner, Martin Kippenberger, wanted to eject her „without any reason whatsoever", and her hand was slit open by a shard of glass in the ensuing chaos, she threw the rest of the glass into his face. According to another version, this event took place at the Café Central where Kippenberger greeted Rat Jenny with the words, "Eh, you cunt!". His encounter with this squatter who eventually emigrated to London inspired Kippenberger to create his work "Dialog mit der Jugend" (dialogue with youth).

Rob Gretton (1953 – 1999)

Ex-DJ und Manager von Joy Division und New Order sowie Teilhaber von Factory Records und des Haçienda-Nachtclubs.

Ex-DJ and manager of Joy Division and New Order, as well as partner of Factory Records and the Haçienda nightclub.

Romy Haag

1948 als Eduard Frans Verbaarsschott in den Niederlanden geborene Sängerin und Nachtclubbesitzerin, die 1974 das Cabaret Chez Romy Haag eröffnete, zu dessen Gästen u.a. Freddy Mercury, Lou Reed, Mick Jagger und David Bowie gehörten, mit dem sie auch befreundet war.

Born in the Netherlands in 1948 as Eduard Frans Verbaarschott, singer and nightclub owner who opened the cabaret Chez Romy Haag in 1974, amongst whose guests included Freddy Mercury, Lou Reed, Mick Jagger and David Bowie, and with whom she was also friends.

Salomé

1954 in Karlsruhe geborener Künstler, der an der Universität der Künste studierte und zu den Neuen Wilden zählt, im Dschungel und im Café Anderes Ufer als Kellner jobbte und 1980 zusammen mit Luciano Castelli die Band Geile Tiere gründete.

Born in Karlsruhe in 1954, an artist who studied at the University of the Arts, and who was part of the New Wild Style, worked in the Dschungel and at the Café Anderes Ufer as a waiter and who, in 1980, together with Luciano Castelli, founded the band Geile Tiere.

Straps-Harry (1907 – 2004)

Der als Harry Toste geborene Travestiekünstler trug vorzugsweise kurze Hosen, Strapse, lange rote Wollstrümpfe und hatte schulterlange grüngelbe Haare, wenn er im Parisiana in der Schöneberger Welserstraße auftrat und Lieder von Zarah Leander sang. Selbst mit 90 Jahren tanzte er noch auf einem Wagen der Love Parade.

Born Harry Toste, a drag queen who liked to wear short trousers, suspenders, long red wool socks and shoulder-length yellow-green hair when he appeared on the stage at the Parisiana on the Schöneberger Welserstraße singing songs from Zarah Leander. At the age of 90, he was still dancing on one of the floats at the Love Parade.

Thierry Noir

1958 in Lyon geborener Maler, der seit 1982 in Berlin lebt und dessen Werke in der East Side Gallery zu sehen sind. Als er 1984 zusammen mit Christophe-Emmanuel Bouchet und Kiddy Citny begann, die Mauer zu bemalen, versuchten vier bewaffnete DDR-Grenzsoldaten ihn zu verhaften, indem sie über den anti-imperialistischen Schutzwall sprangen.

Born in Lyon in 1958, a painter who has lived in Berlin since 1982 and whose work can be seen at the West Side Gallery. As he began to paint the Wall, together with Christophe-Emmanuel Bouchet and Kiddy Citny, four armed border guards from the GDR tried to arrest him by leaping over the anti-imperialistic security wall.

Thomas Wydler

1959 in Zürich geborener Schlagzeuger von Die Unbekannten, Die Haut und Nick Cave and The Bad Seeds.

Born in Zurich in 1959, the drummer for Die Unbekannten, Die Haut and Nick Cave and The Bad Seeds.

Tony Wilson (1950 – 2007)

Britischer TV-Journalist, Gründer von Factory Records und Betreiber des Clubs The Haçienda, der Ende der Achtzigerjahre zum Epizentrum der Madchester-Rave-Szene wurde. Hauptprotagonist des Films *24 Hour Party People,* in dem er von Steve Coogan gespielt wurde.

British TV journalist, founder of Factory Records and operator of the club The Haçienda which became the epicentre of the Manchester rave scene at the end of the eighties. Main character of the film 24 Hour Party People, where he was played by Steve Coogan.

Wayne County

Amerikanischer Travestiekünstler, der in London die Punk-Band Wayne County & The Electric Chairs gründete, sich später in Jayne County umbenannte und als Solokünstlerin auftrat. Im Café Metropol führte er 1980 die *Rock'n'Roll Peep Show* auf und in Rosa von Praunheims Film *Stadt der verlorenen Seelen* spielte sie die Hauptrolle.

American drag queen who founded the London punk band Wayne County & The Electric Chairs, and who later re-named himself Jayne County and appeared as a solo artist. At the Café Metropol he performed in the Rock'n'Roll Peep Show, and played the leading role in Rosa von Praunheim's film Stadt der verlorenen Seelen.

Trini Trimpop und der wahre Heino

Zazie de Paris

WestBam (Maximilian Lenz)

Benannte sich nach dem New Yorker HipHop-DJ Afrika Bambaataa, bevor er im Metropol Platten auflegte, gemeinsam mit Klaus Jankuhn, DJ Dick, Sandra Molzahn und William Röttger (1948 – 2015) das Techno-Label Low Spirit Recordings gründete und die Dortmunder Mayday-Raves veranstaltete. 1984 veröffentlichte er das Manifest *Was ist Record-Art?*, bei den Olympischen Sommerspielen 1988 in Seoul legte er als Resident-DJ im Auftrag des Goethe Instituts in der Kunstdisco auf. Auf dem 2013 erschienenen Album *Götterstraße* arbeitete er u.a. mit Iggy Pop, Bernard Sumner (New Order), Inga Humpe, Kanye West, Richard Butler (The Psychedelic Furs) und Hugh Cornwell (The Stranglers) zusammen.

Named after the New York Hip-Hop DJ Africa Bambaataa before he started playing records at the Metropol who, together with Klaus Jankuhn, DJ Dick, Sandra Molzahn and William Röttger (1948 – 2015) founded the techno label Low Spirit Recordings, and organised the Dortmund Mayday raves. In 1984, he published the manifesto, "Was ist Record Art?" (what is record art?); at the Olympic Summer Games 1988 in Seoul, he was resident DJ at the Art Disco working on behalf of the Goethe Institute. On the album Götterstraße released in 2013, he worked together with Iggy Pop, Bernard Sumner (New Order), Inga Humpe, Kanye West, Richard Butler (The Psychedelic Furs) and Hugh Cornwell (The Stranglers), amongst others.

Wolfgang Müller

1957 in Wolfsburg geborener Künstler, der an der Hochschule der Künste Grafik, Visuelle Kommunikation und Experimentelle Filmgestaltung studierte. Herausgeber des im Merve Verlag erschienenen Manifests *Geniale Dilletanten*, Mitbegründer der Performance-Band Die Tödliche Doris und Autor von Subkultur Westberlin 1979 - 1989.

Born in Wolfsburg in 1957, an artist who studied graphic arts, visual communication and experimental filmmaking at the University of Art. Editor of the Merve publishing house release of the manifesto Geniale Dilletanten, co-founder of the performance band Die Tödliche Doris, and author of Subkultur Westberlin 1979 - 1989.

Zazie de Paris

1970 in Paris als Solange Dymenzstein geborene trans-sexuelle Schauspielerin und Sängerin, die in Peter Zadeks Fallada-Revue *Jeder stirbt für sich allein* und an der Seite von Ute Lemper und Eva Mattes in *Der blaue Engel* im Theater des Westens auftrat. Wirkte u.a. in Spielfilmen von Knut Hoffmeister und Werner Schroeter und zwei Tatort-Folgen mit.

Born in Paris as Solange Dymenzstein, a transsexual actress and singer who appeared in Pater Zadek's Fallada Revue Jeder stirbt für sich allein, and along with Ute Lemper and Eva Mattes in Der blaue Engel in the Theatre of the West. Contributed to feature films, including those of Knut Hoffmeister and Werner Schroeter, as well as to two episodes of Tatort.

Zensor

1953 als Burkhardt Seiler in Berlin geboren. Einst das jüngste Mitglied des SDS und Gründungsmitglied der Roten Garde, eröffnete er 1979 den Plattenladen Zensor in der Belziger Straße, in dessen Keller auch Konzerte mit Mania D, DIN A Testbild, Mittagspause und DAF stattfanden. Gründer der Indie-Labels Marat (1979) und Zensor (1980).

Born in 1953 in Berlin as Burkhardt Seiler. One of youngest members of the SDS and founding member of the Roten Garde, he opened the record shop Zensor in 1979 on the Belziger Straße where concerts with Mania D, DIN A Testbild, Mittagspause and DAF took place in the cellar. Founder of the indie rock labels Marat (1979) and Zensor (1980).

BILDNACHWEIS / PICTURE CREDITS

Horst Blohm — 74/75, 96/97, 151, 154/155

B-Movie — 23 (2), 30/31 (Peter Wensiersky), 34 ▲, 49, 164/165, 171, 174 (Ben Hardyment)

Fritz Brinckmann — 81

Kiddy Citny — 184/185

Anno Dittmer — 71 ▼, 82 ▼, 89, 90, 91, 92, 93, 94, 100, 108/109, 190/191

Peter Gruchot — 8, 58/59, 60 ▲, 63, 65, 66/67, 73, 76/77, 98/99, 102/103, 106 ▲, 113, 114/115, 116/117, 120, 121, 122/123, 126/127, 130/131, 140, 141, 142, 143, 147, 148/149, 192/193, 194/195

Ute Henkel — 139

Knut Hoffmeister — 14/15, 26/27, 28/29, 42/43, 71 ▲, 82 ▲, 106 ▼, 153, 172/173, 177, 183, 189, Polaroids

Kain Karawahn — 34 ▼, 44/45

Mark McNulty — 160 ▼

Eva Maria Ocherbauer — 72, 84/85, 104/105

Picture Alliance — 196

Jim Rakete — 36, 119

Mark Reeder — 19, 20 (4), 51, 53 (2), 160 (2), 161, 162/163, 164/165, 171, 174, 181

Charles Rielly — 56

Dave Rimmer — 160 ▲

William Röttger — 201 ▲

Ilse Ruppert — 10 (5), 13 (5), 25, 37, 38/39, 40/41, 60 ▼, 68/69, 86/87, 125, 128, 132/133, 136/137, 138, 166/167, 178

Irmgard Schmitz — 53 ▼

Hermann Vaske — 52 ▲

Ernst Volland — 16, 46, 54, 78, 110, 144, 156, 168, 186, 204

Die Rechte der einzelnen Fotos liegen beim Herausgeber, beim Autor sowie den Fotografen.

Trotz sorgfältiger Recherche konnten die Urheber der Bilder nicht in allen Fällen ermittelt oder ihre Genehmigung eingeholt werden. Wo dies nicht möglich war, bitten die Herausgeber um Nachsicht. Bei etwaigen Ansprüchen setzen Sie sich bitte mit dem Verlag in Verbindung.

DANKSAGUNG / ACKNOWLEDGEMENTS

Our sincere thanks go to the following photographers who made this book happen.

Wir möchten uns bei allen Fotografen bedanken, die dieses Buch erst ermöglicht haben, insbesondere bei:

Horst Blohm, Fritz Brinckmann, Anno Dittmer, Peter Gruchot, Knut Hoffmeister, Eva Maria Ocherbauer, Ilse Ruppert und Ernst Volland (in memoriam Käthe B.).

▶ Mark Reeder

B-MOVIE LUST & SOUND IN WEST-BERLIN 1979-1989

DIE HOMMAGE AN WEST-BERLINS UNDERGROUND DER 80ER JAHRE

B-MOVIE ist eine Dokumentation über Musik, Kunst und Chaos im wilden West-Berlin der 80er-Jahre. Bevor der eiserne Vorhang fiel, tummelten sich hier Künstler und Kommunarden, Hausbesetzer und Hedonisten jeder Coleur. Die eingemauerte Stadt war ein kreativer Schmelztiegel für Sub- und Popkultur, Geniale Dilletanten und Weltstars. B-MOVIE erzählt die letzte Dekade der geteilten Stadt, von Punk bis zur Love Parade, mit authentischem Filmmaterial und Originalinterviews.
Mit Annette Humpe, Blixa Bargeld, Nena, Nick Cave, David Bowie, Gudrun Gut, Westbam, Joy Division, Zazie de Paris, Die Toten Hosen, Der „wahre" Heino, Einstürzende Neubauten, Die Ärzte, Die Unbekannten, Malaria!, Notorische Reflexe u.v.a.

SÜDDEUTSCHE ZEITUNG: »...WUNDERBAR...GROSSARTIG...«

HOLLYWOOD REPORTER: »AN APPEALING MEMOIR OF A WILD DECADE...«

WELCOME TO THE B-WORLD!

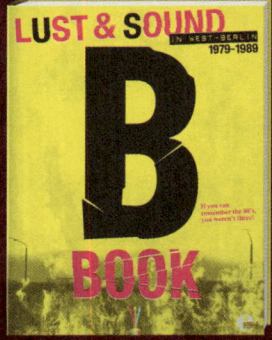

DAS BUCH ZUM FILM!
Spektakulärer Bildband in aufwändiger Ausstattung mit einem exklusiven Text von Mark Reeder in deutscher & englischer Fassung

DER SOUNDTRACK AUF DOPPEL-CD & -VINYL!

B-MOVIE JETZT ALS DVD, BLU-RAY & VOD!

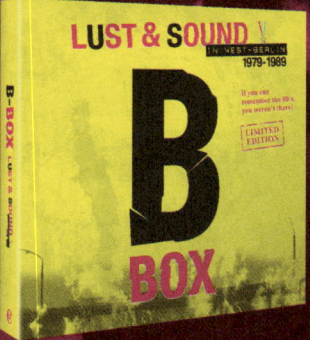

FÜR WAHRE B-KENNER: DIE B-BOX!
Enthält alle Produkte rund um B-Movie:
- den Film als **DVD & Blu-ray**
- den Soundtrack als **Doppel-CD & -Vinyl**
- das **Buch zum Film**
- + zusätzlich kultige **B-Goodies!**